A WARRIOR IN SEARCH OF THE TRUTH.
LANDED HERE AD 28 06 58

Dedication

NELL, A GREAT FOOTBALLER, A LOYAL FRIEND.

David Sutton

Pray Listen

AUSTIN MACAULEY PUBLISHERS™

LONDON • CAMBRIDGE • NEW YORK • SHARJAH

A CIP catalogue record for this title is available from the British
Library.

ISBN 9781787105904 (Paperback)
ISBN 9781787105911 (E-Book)
www.austinmacauley.com

First Published (2017)
Austin Macauley Publishers Ltd.
25 Canada Square
Canary Wharf
London
E14 5LQ

Acknowledgements

BELINDA

MOLLY-ANNE

ROSIE

I LOVE YOU MORE

I LOVE YOU MOST

A True Story

Let's not beat about the bush here. Fact: what I lack in any academic sense I more than make up with my knowledge of how the universe operates, and most importantly, what to do when the shit hits the fan, which it invariably does from time to time.

When I was a wee boy, Batman, Robin and Superman were the heroes of the day to most boys and some girls but for me, Harry Hogg was the dude with all the answers during my childhood; a specialist when it came to minor grazes scrapes and scratches of the knees and hands.

Later vis-a-vis the chickenpox measles and mumps, well let's say he did me proud, put simply he was a bloody hero, although I'm a little embarrassed to admit I could never pronounce his name properly, Higney Renogg was the closest I ever got but neither of us cared. When I finally grew up at the age of 5, my mother revealed everything...she put the wig and costume away and handed all responsibility over to guy called Jesus and his dad called God. Since that time, every crisis has been resolved, every danger passed, major car accidents, health scares, Ankylosing Spondylitis, pneumonia, a Schwannoma and a brain tumour, I only have to ask.

And that's the whole ball of wax, no school, no university, no apprenticeship, no career guarantees happiness, but I'm one of the lucky ones. I was given the key and I've never looked back.

Chapter 1

It's July, and I'm lying back on the Range Rover tailgate with my face levelled up towards the blistering midday sun. Stripped down to my running shorts and trainers, sweat oozes from every pore. My lungs sting in protest as I force down gasps of the hot, dry air in rapid succession after 52.4 minutes of cross-country running. I'm knackered but at the same time heady from the army of endorphins barrelling through my veins.

I am blissfully unaware that in twenty-two minutes precisely, my life will change forever.

This rare moment of peace and tranquillity comes to an abrupt end as my mobile vibrates discreetly to announce the arrival of a text message. I raise my body and swivel my legs around to sit up. Small pools of sweat that have gathered on my chest tumble down my lean stomach while I fumble about in my pocket for the phone. It's a supermarket buyer, an important customer. I press the red button.

I lie back on the Range Rover tailgate and allow myself a faint smile of satisfaction.

Soon enough my heart and lungs are regaining some of their composure and my mind continues to drift into neutral. This is why I enjoy my running so much, no distractions, no one badgering me, not one of my 312 employees need me, no, this is a moment to savour.

Charlie and Fudge, my loyal Labradors, lie sprawled out on the brick weave surface of the courtyard, panting furiously. I guess they run two or three times the distance I do, darting across the fields in irregular directions as they chase down scent after scent. It's great watching them.

Slowly I peel away my trainers with the very last ounces of energy left in my body. As I begin to pluck the spiky corn shoots from my socks, I notice Charlie, the intensity of his breathing and the way his open mouth is mega-drooling with fresh saliva. I wonder whether today's distance has been a bit too much for him. As if sensing my thoughts, he lifts his head off the brick weave surface of the courtyard and grunts, as if to say,

"I'm fucked boss!"

"Well tough shit Charlie, you need to get into shape lad," I chuckle at him as I lie back and stretch out.

A few minutes later I am teetering on the edges of a well-earned and welcome sleep when I hear Danielle's voice from the kitchen window. Reluctantly I raise myself up again, groaning with disapproval.

"I can't hear you Danielle!" I shout back, my voice brimming with impatience. "What did you say?"

"Michelle's just called, there's a man with dogs chasing the girls on our driveway. They're all in tears!"

Well, Danielle is a little prone to exaggeration, even hysteria from time to time, but Michelle, our long serving nanny, suffers neither affliction, in fact she's a little too laid back for my liking. For her to be in tears would indeed suggest one crisis or another.

"Calm down dear," I tell Danielle rather mockingly.

"I'll go over and see what's happening," I turn away from her and slowly walk out of the courtyard and onto the gravel driveway.

The sharp stones beneath my bare feet are like a bed of nails on my sensitive soles I curse out loud with every painful step. To anybody watching me it must look as though I'm dancing over red hot coals, I feel ridiculous as I hobble awkwardly to the end of the driveway.

Once there, I look to my right along our tarmac farm track to see Michelle and the girls on their bicycles. They are all sobbing and ask me if they can go back to the house. I bristle with fury, nobody messes with my family and I brace myself in readiness for some kind of confrontation.

"Of course you can, hurry back, mummy's waiting for you."

Turning to look back along our private road, I can see the guy and his dogs approaching. Instantly, I recognise the broad shoulders and the limp. For reasons I will never understand, this idiot brazenly walks his dogs along our private road, encouraging all four of his mutts to shit on my grass verges. From time to time, when I catch him, I insist he takes the dog turds away in bags, but he always has the gall to deny his dogs are responsible.

"Oy' know whose dogs dunnit, but tha'int none a moyne," he would have me believe.

A few months ago, I came across one of his scruffy half breeds in the process of arching its back and depositing its daily waste on the grass. I stopped the car and, somewhat gleefully, stood beside the animal pointing down to it with a ridiculous smirk of victory on my face. I hoped that would be the end of it. Uncharacteristically, I remember pleading somewhat glibly to him, all Basil Faulty like,

"I have enough to do clearing up after my own dogs," I sighed. "Would you mind terribly removing your dog's excrement from my driveway?"

However, here we are, months later and his four scruffy dogs are frantically chasing one another through the leafy undergrowth beside me, darting wildly between trees and shrubbery, almost in a frenzy of excitement. I could kick myself for being so neighbourly with this moron. My fault for being so soft. All the same, I'd rather not wind this character up if I can avoid it.

"What the fuck is going on?" I ask him in a firm but unaggressive voice. Red faced, he raises his body up to me in some futile gesture of defiance, this fool has no idea what lengths I will go to if I'm threatened.

"Ain't nothin' appnin'," he protests, "Dogs done note wrong, thars' yer kids windin' 'em up."

Blaming my children makes my blood boil, but I stay composed, I can see he is running hot which takes me back a little. Ignoring his posturing I am careful to keep out of this idiot's personal space. All the same, I want rid of this cock as soon as possible.

"Sorry pal, I think it's best for all of us if you walk your dogs somewhere else in future, don't you?"

Now his face is purple with rage.

"Are we goin' somewhere with this?" he growls with a menacing look in his eyes.

I know full well what he's saying, but getting into a fight with this man is not on my agenda this afternoon. I crack a half-smile of indifference.

"I don't want to fall out with you pal, but you need to understand…," I begin, turning to look back to Charlie and Fudge who are barking in our courtyard.

This momentary distraction is enough to bring about a sudden and violent lurch forward by the man as he launches head first towards me. I turn to face him, but there's no time to react. His forehead smashes into my face with such a sickening force it knocks me to the ground. I think I black out, and when I come to my senses lying on the road surface, I am stunned and dazed. In the confusion I look up, bleary eyed, to see my attacker calmly picking up his sun glasses from the grass verge before blowing onto the lenses and putting them back on. He laughs out loud as he walks away.

This carefree gesture enrages me, and I stumble to my feet and go into attack. Despite many years of disciplined Taekwondo training I find myself flailing my arms and fists wildly before collapsing to the ground. Try as I might I can't stand up without falling down again, only able to scream obscenities as this moron, this thug, this coward as he saunters off, throwing his head back in laughter as I begin drifting in and out of consciousness…

Chapter 2

The ambulance crew appear surprisingly ready to believe I have not lost consciousness during or after the attack. I am emphatic about this point despite Danielle and the children insisting that I have indeed been in and out of consciousness several times since the guy dropped me. I realise that to admit this will mean hospital, and for some reason I don't want to go there. I can't think straight at all. The two man crew consider allowing me to remain at home, the only thing on my mind is to reassure Emily and Hannah that I am fine; I've never seen fear and shock in my children's faces before and I am desperate to cheer them up.

A young paramedic leans down to where I lay on the sofa in the kitchen,

"We can't leave you here unless we are sure you haven't sustained any head injuries David." Pause. "Can you tell me the name of our Prime Minister?"

This is crazy! Then it comes to me.

"Tony Brown prick."

There, that told him, I'm hoping upon hope that I've got it right. I'm sprawling out on the sofa in the kitchen, Danielle, Emily and Hannah, the two ambulance crew and a paramedic surround me with fixed expressions.

"Try again David," one of the ambulance crew urges.

I turn my head and look at Danielle for help. She sits down next to me and takes hold of my hand. She is calm, this is the moment I am reminded why I chose my elegant partner. Tall, fair and slim, sophisticated with a classic beauty all of her own. Danielle is fifth generation of the McFunnel brewing dynasty. Not quite the Guinness family, but with fifty-two pubs to control, she is a capable and beautiful woman.

Emily and Hannah both cling to her arm. I can see tears now and Hannah's bottom lip is quivering. I need more time with them; that's all that is going through my mind.

I put on the best smile I can muster and tell them not to worry. They've seen me in fights before, I fear no man, I'm indestructible, I don't go out looking for trouble but I never hesitate to get stuck in if I'm challenged. And I have never, ever been put down like this. The fear in their eyes is unmistakable.

Danielle squeezes my hand and whispers, "The Prime Minister darling."

I turn back to face the softly spoken paramedic who nods his head encouragingly.

"Gordon Blair," I mutter, sensing I might have got it wrong.

Today's date is 24th July. The ambulance doors slam together and I begin to drift in and out of consciousness. Unbeknown to me, my mind and body are beginning to close down and I'm fighting for my life on this calm sunny afternoon.

Chapter 3

I love my dad, George. We're like best mates. He was born in Wimbledon, 1st May 1929. As a child, he can remember the shriek of air raid sirens, the growl of German bombers passing overhead and the smell of brick dust when they left.

He is a product of post war resilience, defiance and determination. When he met April, my amazing mum, he was twenty-one years old, she was only fifteen. Their relationship caused a bit of a scandal at the time, so as soon as they could, they disappeared to Gretna Green and did the honourable thing.

For a long time, they struggled to keep a roof over our heads, but through determination, desperation, a lot of hard graft and Dad's giant pair of cojones, we became fairly wealthy, mum looking after the four of us, two boys and two girls, and Dad a travelling salesman during the daytime and moonlighting in the evenings and at weekends. They are a very cool couple. Very active, full of life, full of energy.

I'm a bit of a hybrid, I've inherited their drive and ambition to succeed. Some would say I'm a little heartless, I don't care, I'm addicted to earning money, I've got an insatiable appetite for the green stuff, I can't get enough of it. Get this, when I eat a bowl of prunes, my favourite fruit, I have to eat them in units of five; Tinker, tailor, soldier, sailor, rich man! And, I have a sort of mosaic poster on my office wall to remind me what I need; jet helicopter, superyacht, penthouse apartment in Monte Carlo, skiing lodge in St Anton.

In my teens, 20s and early 30s, I lived for girls, girls, and more girls. Since then I've been forced to grow up and take life a little more seriously, a business career, marriage, children, have all helped rein me in, but I've always been a rebel at heart with a twinkle in my eye and always game for a laugh. I live it large, if you know what I mean.

Having said all of this, I have had one or two knock backs, the biggest of which happened only recently. This one turned out to be the mother of all setbacks...

Chapter 4

A long time ago I read in one of Donald Trump's biographies that the key to success in business is to surround yourself with good people, trust them and let them get on with it. And that's the way I've run the family business since taking over from Dad. I made a few changes, in particular I headhunted a guy to run the finances, leaving my brother Hugh and I to concentrate on what we're good at; sales and marketing, swilling beer and taking drugs.

A few short years later and the business blossomed, new customers, new product ranges and new packaging took our family business from a £4 million turnover to a solid £20 million medium size business, we started to appear in trade magazines and then national papers, heralded as one of Britain's best performing businesses. We won awards. Order books for the next twelve months were at record levels. We needed help.

Bearing in mind Trump's advice, we promoted our new Finance Manager to Managing Director, trusted him and let him get on with it. Don't get me wrong, he had to submit weekly sales information to me, and monthly management figures to the bank, our accountants and all our directors, but we treat this guy as one of the inner circle. Family.

A few short years pass by before, out of the blue, I receive his voice message on my mobile. It sends a shiver down my spine as I listen to his coarse Middleborough accent,

"I'm resigning with immediate effect. I cannot be contacted. Be lucky."

Baffled, I call Dad. It's a shock, a five star shock, but more than this we begin to analyse what possible motive this man might have to disappear like this. The more we talk, the more uncomfortable we feel. Certain events over the past few months had come to the surface, his purchase of property overseas, his purchase of properties in the north of England, his travel to Asia, his recent ideas and suggestions to leave company funds in Holland and in Denmark where we purchase most of our product, our imaginations soon begin to run away with us.

Chapter 5

It takes forensic accountants a few short weeks to discover the proverbial black hole in our accounts. The business has been bled dry. The only concern the bank has is to recover the missing monies. Our credibility and reputation is of no interest to them, neither are the strong trading relationships built up and nurtured with the major supermarkets over many years. They want their money, and they have no desire to track down our MD.

With uncharacteristic desperation, I make some rather frantic approaches to other companies, our competitors, other banks, even our largest supermarket customer. Nobody it seems, likes the sound of a managing director disappearing and leaving unreliable accounts in his wake. To be honest, I can't blame them.

Over the years, we made hundreds of thousands of pounds' profit for the bank. They called our relationship a 'partnership'. Now it's a case of 'this is where we are'.

The bank has 'no duty of care' or 'moral duty' towards us whatsoever. They go to ground. They vanish and hide behind their 'agents' Grunt Thornybag who set about devouring the business without mercy, raping and pillaging and looting the creation we have nurtured and risked so much for over so many years, rewarding themselves with obscene and wholly disproportionate and unchallenged fees that the law apparently allows them to charge.

Over the next few months, we watch helplessly as company assets and stock are sold off for a pittance. Grunt Thornybag's fees together with legal costs, will reach £1 million before their snouts finally leave the trough. Liquidators, Dross Cornfield, are left a few thousand pounds to snort up their nostrils for a bit of fun.

In times gone by, I remember how banks were trusted and held in high esteem. Now their fat cat bosses and greedy traders have a reputation for being the biggest crooks in the country. Have they no shame?

Donald Trump has since published a new, updated version of his book. His views on people appear to be modified, still emphasising the importance of recruiting the very best candidates for the job, but adding a new and radical caveat, namely, never to take your eye off key individuals and to watch them like a hawk! I guess Trump got burned just like we did.

When I use the term 'set back', I am understating the position somewhat. It's more a full on, gold plated catastrophe as far as I'm concerned. It costs us a small fortune, no, double that and you're somewhere near. I'm eaten up with rage, I want revenge, I want blood. I would happily cut off their balls myself if they had any, and I would make our Ex-MD eat them in a single sitting.

Locked out of our own site as the bank, the administrators and the liquidators enjoy the spoils from our butchered business, is, to say the least, torturous. I'm a nightmare to be around, no fog of self-pity or anything as pathetic as that, just an anger that eats away at my soul. My wife and children have to tread on eggshells around me, I have the stench of defeat lingering in my nostrils and the dry taste of retribution controlling everything I do and say.

Dismal memories of sitting alone beneath the canopy of a giant ash tree in the lush, grassy meadow to the front of our house, haunt me day and night. I have two beautiful daughters, a loving wife, the respect of businessmen internationally, a beautiful Georgian house set in thirty acres of parkland, a nice car in the garage, and more than enough of the green stuff. But it's not enough. I want more, and I ask whoever is out there, God, to give me more.

There's a saying isn't there, 'be careful what you wish for, it may come true'.

But now, with the business destroyed, I'm not likely to have anything of value left. In truth, although the money was good, the business has been like having a Tiger by the tail, constantly bullied and never appreciated by the supermarkets, I have to concede it's been a mug's game.

Weird to think that if all this hadn't happened I would still be on the same boring treadmill with my tongue up the buyers' ignorant arses, dancing to their ever-demanding tune.

Bollocks to the lot of them, now I'm free. I am liberated!

You'd think wouldn't you, that losing a business and a shed load of money would be your worst nightmare. I would anyway. But here I am, beginning to feel some sort of euphoria at sticking two fingers up to the whole hideous supermarket sector. Weird. I can't work out how or why my fury is melting into relief, but I would describe this sensation as an emerging happiness, even, dare I use the word, a form of joy. I am sensing my life is turning around, not in a bad way, but in a good way. Extra weird but it's true.

More than all of this, I don't know it yet, but the demise of the business will not only save my life, but it will save my brother's life into the bargain.

Chapter 6

At thirty-six, my brother is seven years younger than I am, we've grown up more like father and son. For virtually all of our adult lives, we have either lived together or next door to one another, we have shared the same friends, sometimes the same girlfriends, we've socialised in the same circles, fought back to back, partied and holidayed together and worked together. We're tight as tight can be.

It's 28th June, my birthday. I love birthdays, I have a brother-in-law who refuses to celebrate his birthday. He spends the day trying hard to be as miserable and obnoxious as he can. I tell him he's an idiot. Anyway, this particular birthday I have the misfortune to be sitting around our boardroom table with a bunch of cocky administrators, each with gurgling Brummie accents, not a shred of industry knowledge between them, and yet a bizarre belief that every hour of their time is worth £500. Jokers.

Today there are four mobile phones lying on the table top, ready for action. When one of them starts to vibrate, we all tip forward on our high backed executive leather seats to see who is most urgently needed. My lips crack a narrow smile as I see my brother's name flashing up on my screen. It's been a while since we've talked together, which is unusual, so I stand up and turn away from the long glass table,

"Waaaas eeeerp amigo?"

I glance backwards wearing a thinly disguised smile and I can sense the disapproval as it fizzles through the stale air towards me. Pens bounce down onto paper pads and bodies are pressed back into their seats, ties are loosened. These big shots have no empathy, no emotion and no comprehension of the pain I feel right now. To destroy a perfectly good business, BECAUSE THEY CAN. They know the man responsible, but choose not to pursue him. Money. They are here for money. I'm beginning to understand how dangerous the stuff is.

I walk away from the Spanish Inquisition, effectively pissing on Grunt Thornybag's parade for once,

"I'm in trouble."

Without turning to explain myself, I simply carry on walking out of the meeting room, down a flight of steps and out into the car park. I drive off at speed, tyres squealing as I thread my way through the queue of waiting lorries.

"Where are you Hugh, what's happened?"

"Home, Mum and Dad are on their way," he splutters, straining to clear his throat.

"Don't worry, I'll be with you in less than twenty minutes."

I'm not sure what to expect when I get back. The main difference between my brother and me is that I know when to stop partying. I'm guessing this is somehow connected to all of this.

When I arrive at The Stables, a converted, single storey brick building originally used for farm horses, Dad welcomes me at the front door. He is a very distinguished and good looking man, I hope I look as good as he does when I'm his age. Today his tanned face beneath his cropped grey hair is creased with this new stress, he looks shattered.

"How's the boy?" I ask.

"I'll let Hugh tell you, come in son"

Hugh is lying on the sofa beneath a crumpled duvet. Mum is perched on the end, she looks pale and is wringing her delicate bony hands together. I kiss her on her forehead and tell her not to worry. I walk past her and sit next to my bro. I take hold of his warm hand. He is gently sobbing into a velvet cushion but turns his head to look up at me. I am shocked to see how his face looks so puffy and his nose so red and swollen,

"You look shit, lad," I tell him.

Over mugs of hot tea, he takes us through the last few days.

Every month or so he meets up with a group of friends whose sole purpose is to perform ever more daring feats of stupidity; base jumping, skydiving in wing suits, cliff jumping, all the types of things that put you in mortal danger, you name it, it's on their list. Sadly, but inevitably, road racing on powerful motorbikes has put an end to one of his friends' lust for excitement. My brother puts it down to the effects of drugs and alcohol.

"None of us drink excessively or use drugs all the time," he sobs.

"But enough to lose your edge Hugh," I tell him.

He's distraught at losing another close friend,

"It's such a waste," he keeps repeating, "I'm checking in to rehab in Cape Town for a couple of weeks. I'm finished with extreme, life is too precious...too fucking precious."

Considering half the population of the civilised world are either in rehab or cleaning up their act with the help of psychiatrists or psychologists, Hugh's reaction is understandable and we help him pack.

Chapter 7

The administrators have locked us out of our own site here in sunny Suffolk. Warehouses stand empty, acres of covered structures used for production and packing are being destroyed by vandals. Our pleas to get back onto the site fall on deaf ears, tens of thousands of plants are stolen every day, it's a free for all. Millions of tender young plants perish. Where are the Grunt Thornybag whiz-kids you may be asking yourself, well they don't set foot on our site that's for sure. In a very short time, the repair bill is £500,000 not including those scandalous fees. And get this, the law protects the administrators against any liability whatsoever.

For the first time in a long long while, I have time to myself. I ponder, I ponder about what has been and about what will be. I am forced to spend time with my wife and children, and I have to admit this brings me a new world of pleasure as I reconnect with each of them. My instincts tell me I should be after the bastard responsible for all of this, chasing him down, getting my money back and breaking his fingers his arms and his fucking legs. Each time I think like this, a voice in my head tells me to relax and enjoy my new life with Danielle and the girls.

Voices in my head! Am I going mad? Am I going soft? I've just lost so much yet my life feels, well, so much richer.

This is all messed up.

Days and weeks pass by. It's late in the afternoon, it's a weekday and I'm scoffing a bowl of cold porridge on my own in the kitchen after the day's run. 54.5 minutes. I know I can do better. For some inexplicable reason, the TV is on and I am drawn into a story about a British neurosurgeon who for the last 15 years has dedicated himself to his patients here in England, and also to the growing number of men, women and children in the Ukraine suffering from brain tumours where it's virtually impossible for most of the population to afford a consultant, let alone the pioneering life-saving surgery and treatment needed to deal with them.

This man just gives. His time, his money, his feelings, his expertise, his love, everything he has he gives to others.

The cameras follow him on a typical visit to the dark grey continent, as this desperately sad story begins to unravel, it's impossible to miss each painful expression on the surgeon's face as he wearily tells desperate parents their young child has only months to live and when he tells a beautiful twenty-three year old student she will shortly be losing her sight for the five short years he predicts she has left.

Cut to a children's ward, the surgeon is sitting in the half light on the edge of a bed where a small child lies motionless post-surgery, only a blood stained bandage around his or her head gives the brain tumour away.

Gently taking hold of the child's small hand, this wonderful medicine man can't hide the joy he is feeling, hope stretching his worn, wrinkled face, and then comes his gravelly voice giving way to words of the child's possible recovery,

"I have high hopes for this young lady," is all he will admit to.

The tears welling up in my eyes begin to bounce over my cheek. My problems are nothing compared to the agony these people face every day. A sense of shame hangs over me like a black cloud.

Cut to outdoors. Drizzle paints the day grey. Our man is standing bolt upright below a large black umbrella. He is uncomfortable with all this attention and his body language is stiff and awkward.

From behind camera a quiet voice asks him to sum up his own work and aspirations and beliefs.

Slowly he removes his round-rimmed tortoise shell glasses, slides them into his raincoat pocket and looks directly into the camera lens as if looking deep into my soul, then he begins speaking in his granite-like tone of voice,

"Well," he begins before pausing for thought, "what are we if we don't try to help others?" he asks.

There is a longer pause, as if he is going over the question one more time, checking to see if there could be any other conclusion, but nothing new comes.

"We are nothing," he answers with a sombre tone of indignation, his gaze still tunnels deep into my soul.

He replaces his glasses, turns away from camera and walks slowly back through the graveyard which is lined with small new headstones.

For a moment, my mind is frozen. We are nothing if we don't help others, how right, how profound. This, rather blunt conclusion, coming after the horror, the pain, the sadness, and also the glimpses of joy and hope this programme contains, forces me to ask myself the question. What am I doing with my life?

Chapter 8

By the time my brother comes back to the UK, almost a year has passed. He's found a real purpose to his life in Cape Town, helping those in need, qualifying as some sort of paramedic and addiction counsellor, generally leading what he calls 'a Christian way of life'.

He comes back a new man. He's morphed back into the brother I knew a long time ago, content, fresh faced, happy-go-lucky, full of kindness, up for a laugh. He has no doubt that his faith in God has transformed his life.

I must admit, I prayed he would come back more settled. But I never dreamt he would come back such a calm and satisfied individual. He understands why he led such a hair-raising way of life. Business rewarded him with plenty of money but little satisfaction, and little enjoyment. Giving to others is his thrill now.

Over the next days and weeks, we chat incessantly about life, I love Hugh's positivity, the strength in his voice, and I can see the lines of happiness that crease his chuckling face as it did all those years ago.

But I'm a lousy Christian. I hardly ever go to church. I do believe in God because it's perfectly logical that someone created everything. Whenever I've found myself in the shit I pray, and somehow I get through it. My conversations with Hugh force me to look at myself, and I don't like what I see.

It's bizarre to think that the loss of our business and the knowledge my bro has picked up from his spell in South Africa, have collectively brought peace and happiness into all our lives. The more I sit around and mull over the meaning of life, the more I pick up the faith vibe. I like it.

More pondering. I am beginning to think clearly now, I have come to the conclusion that business only ever gave me pleasure in the early days, working shoulder to shoulder with my father in the fields and in the office and all for a pittance. As it grew and expanded and became a much more sophisticated business employing around one hundred and then two and three hundred people of all creeds and colours, I was dragged onto a treadmill that I couldn't get off. So now, to have a second chance at getting life right, to be given the time to discover what makes me tick, well, it's a miracle.

My whole world as I know it is slowly being dismantled, not by me but by the crazy things that are happening to me and around me.

I've come to the conclusion that if there is a God or a creator or a superior power in the universe, it must mean that absolutely anything is possible. Anything at all.

You'd think I would feel vulnerable even fearful not knowing how my future will take shape. None of it, don't ask me why because I don't understand it, but something does tell me to concentrate on my fitness. I run harder and longer, across fields, along the headlands, and over the top of sea banks. Charlie and Fudge our loyal Labradors run with me, darting across the fields in irregular directions as they chase down scent after scent. The peace and tranquillity of the outdoors slams my mind into neutral...

Chapter 9
Addenbrooke's

My family suffer long agonising days and longer more exhausting nights waiting, praying and desperately hoping that I will survive. Doctors are confused, their prognosis seems to change from day to day, first it's a stroke then it's a brain haemorrhage and other terrifying possibilities.

"If David pulls through, he's likely to have a degree of brain damage," one doctor warns my family as they hover around my bed in Addenbrooke's Critical Care Unit.

Chapter 10

By the time I surface beneath the calm half-light of Addenbrooke's critical care unit, the outside world has given up on me, but my family never doubted for one moment that their prayers would be answered.

I am trying hard to open my eyes, all of the lifelines and breathing apparatus have been disconnected, and my stomach is churning like a washing machine. Suddenly, and without warning, I throw up three waves of bright green vomit, with each wave comes a real sensation of coming alive. I am frantically struggling to sit up in bed, I don't know where I am or why I am here. I can't sit up because there's a weight across my chest, I later discover it's a nurse called Greg, and with unhesitating devotion and compassion he is using all of his weight to pin me back down onto the bed as I struggle to breathe and to fight my way back to life.

Another wave of the vile, bright green matter erupts, this time over Greg's face his neck and his forearms. In any other circumstance, I would have laughed out loud but here, now, I'm deeply embarrassed. Finally I manage to take in a gasp of air, before drifting back into the darkness again. Feels like I'm half dead half alive. No pain here.

When I wake, in the dusky light, the ward, holding ten or twelve patients I guess, is eerily still and calm, the silence only interrupted by the careful movements of nursing staff quietly going about their business as life support machines hiss and click all around me.

My eyes can't focus properly, but I can make out the mummified figure of a body lying horizontally on a bed opposite my own. It is wrapped head to toe in white swaddling, just like you'd see in 'Carry on Doctor' or 'Tomb Raiders III'. He or she is attached to the life support apparatus and doesn't move.

This new world scares me. The old David, invincible, cocky, confident and self-assured, has been stripped down to the bare bones. I'm helpless. And I begin trembling with an unfamiliar and cold fear. I hope I'm back in the world I came from, if I am, I'll know there is a God, but I can't sense whether I'm back or whether I'm in heaven or even in hell. I don't have enough energy to hold my eye lids open and I drift back to sleep.

The shrill of an urgent alarm brings me to my senses. I manage to force one eyelid open, only a couple of millimetres, but enough to make out the shape of the mummy straight ahead of me. The thing is coming alive, desperately clawing at its face to tear away the breathing apparatus, flailing with both arms and legs as two nurses glide across and begin to force it down, first the arms then torso and finally the legs.

I think this must be hell.

Still clamping it down onto the bed, the nurses gently yet firmly plead for 'Paul' to calm down as his burned body writhes and jerks and fights against the pain. A doctor in a white coat arrives at the scene and gives him a shot intravenously. Paul's crazy panic begins to subside as suddenly as it had begun, and in its place the calm semi silence of muffled clicks and hum's returns.

No sense of time here, wherever here is, but at some point, I'm vaguely aware that I've been transported to another place. There's more light, I sense there are fewer people, and I hear the voices, first Danielle, then Hugh, my dad and my mum. Relief is not a word strong enough to describe how I felt when I heard those voices.

Most of the time I sleep beneath a soothing cocktail of painkillers and other drugs that disable and neutralise my mind and body. I am mostly unaware of my family's constant bedside vigil also of the tender care I receive around the clock.

Until one day, when I half open my eyes and see the smiling figure of a brown-skinned nurse, I guess she is Indian, no more than nineteen or twenty years old, standing perfectly still at the end of my bed. She has a warm, wide smile with perfectly white teeth and as she notices my eyelids opening, she begins to move very slowly around the bed to talk to me. I notice how her calm gaze through those disarming nut-brown eyes never leave my own. I am mesmerised, attracted to her like a moth to a flickering light. Her lips are partly open, stretched into a narrow smile.

"Are you feeling better today?" she asks in a gentle voice. I nod back to her as she sits down on the seat beside me. She is holding a Bible, it's blue, a bit tatty, and looks old and well thumbed.

"David, would you like me to read you something?" she asks in a voice as sweet as honey. I give a shallow nod.

When she leaves, it feels like I'm suspended inside a bubble of peace and tranquillity. I hadn't seen her before, and despite looking out for her over the following days and weeks, she doesn't come back to see me again.

Chapter 11

Anybody who spends time in hospital would understand me when I say one day merges into the next, only a bland meal or a visit from family or a medical procedure interrupts the monotony. Today, it's a medical procedure that lightens up the atmosphere.

A plump nurse with eyes set too close together is whispering to me in one ear, but her English is impossible to understand. I feel a bit stupid, it's early in the day, I think, and I'm still drowsy from the drugs I took last night.

She whips my sheet back with gusto which immediately gets my attention and she happily continues to chatter in her strong Polish or Lithuanian or Russian accent. Only one word stands out. Catheter. I turn my head to face her and notice how her pupils are dancing about like mosquitoes, I can sense this is building up to something. It is.

Suddenly, and without warning, an electrifying pain shoots down from my bladder to the tip of my knob, a searing, burning pain that literally suspends my body above the mattress for what feels like minutes as she struggles to pull the rubber pipe back through my pecker.

This is unbearably painful (I'm a man), and when it's finally over, I open my eyes and see the thick rubber pipe on the metal trolley. The pipe is so wide I can't help wondering how on Gods earth they got it up there.

Strange as it sounds, as she retreats out of the ward, this rather tender procedure has evoked a sense of progress and of me getting better.

Chapter 12

Later in the afternoon my consultant arrives at my bedside. He is a rugged, good looking man, over six feet tall, with a flatness to his nose and ears like that of a battle-hardened rugby player. He is a serious man and I try to make light of the experience I had this morning, but he's having none of it. He wants to concentrate on the more serious issues at hand, and this is the first real chat we've had together,

"The blow to your head, David, may have temporarily starved your brain of oxygen," he begins, "typically this can result in a stroke or one or two other consequences."

Great. In my mind, I am already refusing to believe anything he is saying.

"And there is something else on your scans that I would like to take another look at."

I don't know what to say, what else can there be? He isn't finished.

"I'm pretty sure it's nothing malignant but we need to keep an eye on it, possibly do a biopsy in two or three months' time to see if there's any movement. I've organised an MRI scan for later today."

He throws me a narrow smile and we exchange a nod of heads before he turns and leaves the ward.

If it's not enough to have a near death experience, now he's talking about something else, using those dreaded words malignant and biopsy. My shield of invincibility has been torpedoed broadside, cancer happens to other people, not me. A biopsy? Malignant? This is too extreme. Mad.

Disbelief pumps through my veins like shards of glass, so fast and furiously that I am super alert, no trace of any type of emotional breakdown, tears simply don't come.

I lie cold and motionless on my bed and begin to pray. And pray. And pray. What would you do? I'm terrified.

"Please God, I beg of you, please please please don't take me away from Emily and Hannah and Danielle, they need me, I need them. This is way too early, I've got so much to do. Please, please don't let this be it."

My prayers come automatically, whenever a crisis comes, I pray. And believe me when I tell you, I've had more than my share of dramas and scrapes, and my prayers have always been answered. Not necessarily in a way that I expect, but always in a way that gets me through.

When I come down from the scan, Danielle, Hugh, Mum and Dad, my sisters, Louise and Rachel are all waiting for me in the ward, each one of them pale-faced with worried eyes glistening over weak smiles.

"It's great they are being so thorough," I remind them, to which they all chortle in agreement.

There's only so much tittle tattle we can muster between us before tackling all of this head on.

"Don't worry, I'll get over this, it's all going to be fine," I tell everybody with an upbeat tone to my voice,

Each of them in turn reciprocates that positivity tenfold, it's as if we were all half asleep and suddenly now we are all fired up like a well-disciplined team in the changing rooms before the big match.

Chapter 13

Most of the time these days I'm dog tired, the air is thick and warm in here, and I pass my time drifting in and out of sleep. Only the door swinging open creates any movement in this stale, stuffy atmosphere and this afternoon it is my surgeon who throws the door open and strides into the room. Danielle, Hugh and my parents are all here, either dozing or half-asleep and his entrance startles all of us. He strides up to my bedside with purpose in his step, wearing a more serious expression on his face than before.

"David I'd like you to go home for a week and come back for a biopsy," he blurts out, "I need to know what I'm dealing with here."

As if in a tearing hurry to get somewhere, he nods to everyone in the room, turns on his heels and marches out of our lives again.

The change of tempo compared to his previous plan, well to say the least, unnerves all of us. It's one of those surreal moments when you have to pinch yourself to check it's not a terrible nightmare. I tumble back into an uncomfortable sleep and when I wake up, my family are huddled together talking in whispers.

"Let's get you home son," my dad tells me.

Considering I am about to have a hole drilled into my skull the size of a fifty pence piece, and a chunk cut away from my brain, I am relaxed and calm during the next week. My brother is mostly responsible for this as he talks to me about what he learnt in South Africa. The Bible is full of miracles, positivity and hope, and I feel as if somebody or something is using him as an instrument to reassure me that I will recover from all of this. Sounds a bit cranky, but it's true.

Chapter 14

"David, can you hear me? David, wake up please."

This goes on and on and on. When I slowly open my eyes, the voice is still talking.

"Tell me David, on a scale of one to ten how is the pain?"

A man's face comes into focus, he is oriental looking, dressed in green and wearing a tight fitting Theatre cap. The word 'pain' jolts me into the real world. I remember him from the pre-op room, he's the anaesthetist.

"Ten," I assure him as my senses begin to surface above the anaesthetic. I close my eyes to shield them against the bright white lights of the recovery room.

"David, it's good news, our tests show a grade two."

I have no idea what grade two means, but if the guy is telling me good news, I'm not about to argue with him, good news is good news, and as extra morphine begins to pump through my veins, I drift back into a pain free sleep.

A few more days' recuperation in Addenbrooke's and I'm winging my way back across the Fens with my head hanging out of the car window, taking in the warm summer air. Morale is high, Louise and Hugh talk incessantly about their research into grade two brain tumours and the general consensus is one of positivity and optimism.

Chapter 15

21st August and I am sort of looking forward to meeting my surgeon to discuss what, if any, treatment is necessary. I am not expecting anything complicated and the mood is relaxed, so I ask my circle of protection to stand down. Despite this, Danielle, Hugh, Mum and Dad, have all insisted on coming, so we all plan to have a slap-up lunch in Cambridge after the meet.

A small consultant's office on the ground floor of the hospital has been allocated for our meeting, much too small for our needs, but we manage to perch on table corners and share seats while we wait for my consultant.

A few minutes later, a new, younger face enters the room, his head is immersed in a pile of papers and what looks like MRI images. When he lifts his face and looks around the crowded room, he becomes rather flustered.

"Morning, my name is Bruce. Duncan is away on holiday, but I am one of his team."

He sprays the words around the room like machine gun fire. His tone is noticeably cold and detached.

I look over to my father and we exchange frowns. Bruce nervously sinks his head back into the file he is carrying and then strides over to light up the scans of my brain. He tilts his head upwards looking closely at the images for a moment and then turns back into the room,

"Mr Sutton?" He enquires, scanning the room,

"Guilty as charged mi Lord," I perk up. No response from Bruce. What's with all this negativity?

Turning slightly to address me, he begins to read out loud from the paperwork. His delivery reminds me of a bumbling barrister, having frantically read the case bundle only moments before entering court, not fully understanding the details, just muddling along as best he can. He briefly reels off various extracts from my consultant's notes before raising his gaze towards my own.

"Do you have any questions Mr Sutton?"

The question hangs in the air, it's almost comical, I look around to check whether anyone else gets the picture. A full set of blank expressions gives me the answer

"I didn't really understand a word you said," I tell him with a hint of humour in my voice, "in really simple terms what's the next step?"

His demeanour takes on a hint of frustration, even dare I say, impatience. He turns back to the grey images lurking behind him,

"Look at this," he snaps, his tone full of accusation. We are all a little startled, and sit up straight.

"I can't operate on this!" he gasps, tapping the backlit images impatiently with his index finger, "Well I could, if you want me to, but it would be dangerous, very dangerous indeed."

There is a pause in the room. I look around and see glum, confused expressions and we all sense there is something yet to come but none of us know what to say to this cold fish.

"This is a Glioblastoma multiforme," he pronounces, almost in a mocking tone of voice, "a grade four."

He is still talking *at* us, as if we understand what he's talking about. Tapping the images with a pen he finishes his dismal lecture.

"See these, they're like sponges, impossible to remove safely." His tone has a mix of fear and defeat.

No one in the room knows what to say, but I find myself asking the obvious question,

"So, if we don't operate, what do we do? What's plan B?"

He shakes his head, his lips narrow, and he shrugs his shoulders.

"Typically in a case like this I would expect someone to survive up to six months."

I don't listen to anything else, we are all in a spin as we exit the small room in single file, each giving the man a firm handshake with our heads held high with dignity.

Once in the corridor we scatter into groups of one and two, my mum has to be supported by Dad, I have my arm around Danielle's shoulder and ahead of me, Hugh's giant shoulders are heaving up and down as he sobs into a handkerchief. For some reason, watching Hugh breakdown like this, such a big brave tough man, makes me determined not to let my family down.

"Group hug!" I tell everybody in a super-positive voice, and we all shuffle together. I am the only one not in tears and my voice is steady and strong.

"All of you, listen. I am not going anywhere for a long time yet," I find myself telling them. Something inside me is telling me I have nothing to fear, it sounds crazy but it is true, "I'm going to get over this, I promise, please don't worry."

I realise I'm going need a miracle, but something deep inside assures me a miracle is on its way.

Chapter 16

We need a second opinion, and fast. My parents, brother and sisters sit around our patio table, beneath the shade of our giant cream parasol, to research my condition and to make contact with other oncology experts around the world. Life as we know it, has been slammed into neutral and parked. All of us have only one thing in mind and finally all roads have led to a Professor Prada of the Royal Marsden Hospital London. He is the number one man in the world for my condition.

It's 27th August, time is ticking away but I remain alive. We all take a train down to London for the two o'clock appointment with El numero uno. We are all brimming with positivity, and decide that Louise should be our spokesman today. She qualified as a barrister and is a solicitor now, she is used to public speaking and we may need her abilities to defend us against any negativity the professor might try to throw at us.

I had a dream last night, I was injured and someone was carrying me over their shoulder in the heat of battle.

At King's Cross we take two taxis across the city to the Royal Marsden. Twenty minutes later we are standing outside the hospital. We are very early for the meeting, just as Dad always likes to be, so we set about finding somewhere close by to eat a light lunch.

Sauntering around the corner of the hospital, we soon come across a small restaurant in the quiet backstreets, away from the waves of rattling taxis lurching from traffic light to traffic light and away from the crazy dispatch riders hurtling through the city on their well-worn motorbikes.

We are seven in number, and take up almost half of the dining area. The atmosphere is intimate, the room is light and airy and the food is a mix of fresh salads, pasta and sea food. We could be in the Mediterranean.

We fit nicely around the oval table and order fresh pasta and fish which we swill down with Pinot Grigio and ice cool water. We hatch a cunning plan;

We can't afford to allow anybody to burst our bubble of positivity, if we get a sniff of negativity, Louise will nip it in the bud and we'll hightail it out of there.

So we finish our leisurely lunch and march back to the hospital with purpose in our stride. All that comes into my mind now is something Hugh pulled out of the Bible, something like; God has a plan for me, not a bad plan but a good plan. I repeat it in my mind over and over again.

So we all troop into yet another small, white room, this time with our defences up. I don't hear any footsteps behind me but I sense we are being followed.

Sure enough, I turn to see a short, bespectacled man no more than 5'8" I guess, wearing a timid smile. He stops at the opened door and coyly takes a head count before apologising profusely for the shortage of seats. He turns on his heels and comes back with a chair on each arm and a colleague behind him carrying another one.

When we are all seated, he remains standing with a shy smile on his face as he looks around the room. I notice he is wearing what looks like a very expensive pair of blue suede moccasins, Prada I guess, I nearly bought a similar pair from Russell and Bromley, now I wished I had.

"My name is Paul," he announces in a calm and welcoming voice, "who's the victim?" he asks light-heartedly. His whole manner is immediately disarming and comforting.

"Guilty as charged," I pipe up, throwing back a wry smile as he walks towards me with his arm outstretched.

He holds our handshake for what seems a very long time, and then he makes his way around the room introducing himself to each one of us.

He is carrying a grey folder, presumably containing all my grisly medical details. It's impossible to read the expression on his face, it is obvious he is a gentle man, a little shy, certainly a modest man, with a mischievous glint in his eye which we all warm to from the get go.

"Right, I have studied all of your scans."

We all look towards Louise, I want to encourage her to warn him now about popping our bubble of hope and positivity but I can't catch her eye. I'm tempted to cut in but it's too late as he continues to talk. What this man says next will determine my future, if I have a future.

"Let me tell you now," he begins, in a firm voice clothed in velvet,

"I do not agree with this."

He is holding up a letter of some sort and shaking it with contempt.

Nobody in the room utters a word.

We have all been praying with all our might for a miracle, someone to tell us this has all been some sort of dreadful mistake. Is this man about to deliver a miracle or

56

is he about to give worse news? The suspense and tension hangs in the room like an early morning mist, this is an all or nothing moment that stretches time like an elastic band.

"If this represents the scale of good to bad," he begins, holding his small hands a shoulder width apart, "and this end is good and that end is bad," he explains, "in my opinion, I consider you to be at the very top of the good end," he announces confidently.

Not one of us can speak. When I entered this room, it was as if I was strapped to the table ready for execution, hoping and praying for a reprieve, a stay of execution at the last minute. Suddenly, it's as though the soft black hood has been removed, and the mouth piece and straps that are pinning my body down in anticipation of the killer poison being fed through my veins, are being withdrawn. Could it be that God is giving me a second chance?

"I am not denying a problem exists, but there are very effective treatments now, and more in the pipeline, all of which could enable you to have a perfectly normal life expectancy."

Only recently my mother confessed that she had been diagnosed with a terminal condition many years ago. Like me, she was given just months to live. At the time she told none of us, keeping that terrifying secret to herself, determined to protect us all from that devastating prognosis for as long as possible. She too prayed for more time, she used all the prayers she had in her. A few weeks later she travelled to London for a second opinion and was told that the original doctor had completely misdiagnosed her condition. She believed then and she believes now, that a miracle touched her and she hasn't stopped thanking God ever since.

We travel home exhausted, relieved and fortified with hope. At night, I lie awake going over and over the conversation with Professor Prada.

"Nobody can tell you how long you will live, far too many variables, age, tumour types, the benefit of your early detection," and his parting comment, "I want you running many more of those marathons in the future David."

Back at home everything he told us today spins around and around in my head until finally, a calm sleep takes over. I have no control or influence over what is happening to me.

Chapter 17

After the euphoria of London, on 3rd September, I decide to write to Professor Prada, or Angel Prada as we have nicknamed him;

Dear Paul,

You may remember a rather unruly family coming to you on Wednesday, 27th August, asking for a second opinion in relation to a prognosis of my brain tumour.

Only days before, we had been shattered by the comments made by the consultant at Addenbrooke's hospital, and whilst we are the strongest and most optimistic of characters normally, we were struggling with the hopelessness that he left us with.

Before we trooped into your room, we had all been praying for something, however faint, anything, a kernel of hope that I can beat this thing and live a normal life. I have to admit, we were prepared to hear one colleague covering for another. How cynical we are all becoming.

They say 'God moves in mysterious ways', don't they? To hear your positive prognosis, well, I can't begin to tell you how that feels.

I've heard it said that 'hope is the best antidote to fear', and you delivered that in spades.

May God bless you and peace be with you, thanks
again.

David

Chapter 18

It's not many days before we all troop back to Addenbrooke's to meet the professor's protégé, Sarah.

When she appears, I am struck by her miniature features and tiny proportions. She is a cute 5'2" I guess, in her 30s (just!), and she speaks confidently and with authority.

"This combination of treatment, using Temozolomide together with targeted radiotherapy, is a revolutionary combination, prolonging life expectancy possibly exponentially," she begins, oozing with Prada bravado.

I want to hug this woman.

"I am going to beat this, I intend to live to be a fit old man who enjoys playing with his grandchildren." Her lips widen into a narrow smile of approval. I feel I'm on a bit of a roll so I give her the whole nine yards.

"God has a good plan for me, I know it, when can we get started?"

She gives a toothy smile and continues.

"David, you are at the top of my A list," she quips.

"First, I need you measured for a face mask. This protects the rest of your brain from the radiotherapy. Then we are ready for a six week course of radiotherapy and chemotherapy, five sessions a week."

"Bring it on," I tell her enthusiastically.

"Be aware, there are cases when a patient can't tolerate the Temozolomide David, if that's the case we will move to plan B," Sarah tells me reassuringly. I'm not interested in any plan B.

"Give me all you've got, I'm a survivor," I tell her doggedly.

Chapter 19

The evenings are beginning to draw in earlier now. Some days, from morning to night, grey clouds hover low overhead and drivers have to use their headlights all day long.

Within the gloom, I notice how this new stress is ageing Mum and Dad, but I can't allow myself any negative latitude, I have to concentrate on positivity, positivity, positivity.

My mobile phones are crammed full of messages, I wish I could say they're from various caring friends and colleagues, but the truth is that virtually all of them are business calls. The early messages have a friendly tone, and gradually their frustration turns into anger and bitterness, some are even threatening. I delete 'all contacts' and throw the phones away.

What a fool I've been. Taking so much for granted, treating people like shit, risking everything.

Despite all of this, someone must be looking over me. The head butt, out of the blue, to a very specific area of my cranium gave me the all-important early detection of the tumour.

The collapse of the business gave me the opportunity to get super fit, and doctors tell me this has been key to my survival after the attack.

My surprise decision to abstain from alcohol many months ago has left my liver clean as a new pin, again doctors tell me the condition of my liver is vital to the success of the Temozolomide.

My very existence is down to this fantastic cocktail of weird and wonderful events and circumstances, all this weirdness is saving my life. How could I not believe there's someone up there pulling the strings.

Chapter 20

So here I am, after fighting the effects of the assault, and now, preparing for the next battle to defeat a brain tumour.

Mum and Dad spend weekdays with us and travel back to the coast at weekends. There's more than enough room for them in our house and they bring a feeling of solidarity into our home. We all love the new smells of home cooking wafting through the downstairs rooms and the bowls of washed fruit out on the kitchen table to pick at. Mum insists on us all eating porridge and poached eggs in the mornings, including Hugh who marches round from his converted barn next door. It feels like the nerve centre or the campaign headquarters from where we are fighting for my life.

Hugh gets into the habit of texting me encouraging messages last thing at night. Mostly these are excerpts from the Bible.

"Remember Dave, the Lord is by your side every inch of the way, so you have nothing to worry about. You are never alone. He has the power to restore, all you have to do is believe. Sleep well, love ya x."

Last night it was another gem from the Bible.

"Jeremiah 29 Chapter 11; I say this because I know what I am planning for you, I have good plans for you, not plans to hurt you. I will give you hope and a good future."

It's difficult to describe the effect this is all having on me. Listening to Hugh and thinking about these extracts from the Bible, I feel myself changing. Sounds weird I know. Sure, I'm in the shit and most people in my position need something positive to cling onto, but I'm no fool. I know I am changing. How can I describe it? It's like I'm falling in love, a warm inner excitement, butterflies in my stomach; uplifting stuff I can tell you. If I told you I'm falling in love with Jesus, you might think I'm nuts.

All the books I am reading now are inspirational stories about real people overcoming seemingly insurmountable problems. There's a common thread running through most of these incredible victories against all the odds. A belief in God and Jesus.

And I'm picking up a lot of practical advice such as, in my case, actually in everybody's case but particularly when you have a dodgy cell or two; avoid refined sugar at all costs and eat organic foods whenever you can. The sugar thing sounds horrendous, most delicious things contain refined sugar, but Danielle has already discovered a whole new world of delicious raw chocolate bars, chai seeds, healthy grains and nuts, just for me.

It's Sunday night and I get a call from a friend, David Greystone. I met him about a year ago, before all of this. It's true to say we hit it off straight away. He has a lot of energy, a wicked twinkle in his eye and is always interested to hear what people have to say. He's bright, a city analyst, who works his arse off and plays just as hard. Lately he's had to tone things down a lot. A few years ago he was diagnosed with a tumour on his heart.

"They gave me a month," he told me when I met him, "but they hadn't factored in the most important parts of the equation," he said knowingly, "me…and God. I'm a stubborn bugger and I wasn't about to go anywhere," he chuckled.

That was nearly 7 years ago he still boasts about having 'plenty left in the tank' although he is philosophical about the future. "I'll go when I'm needed, could be today, tomorrow, next year I don't know," he admits.

I've noticed he ends our conversations with a 'God Bless', and he once told me that he values God's help immensely. I never took much notice before all of this, but now it's another shred of evidence that backs after up the whole God thing. Maybe I'm not going mad after all. I've followed my instincts all my life and right now everything is telling me Jesus is real and the messages that come into my thoughts are real.

Our conversation tonight is very typical. He wants both of us to climb Everest. It's a hare brained idea, completely mad but I humour him. These days he struggles to climb his own staircase without getting out of breath and when I point this out he cackles and splutters down the telephone. What a dude.

Chapter 21
It's Monday, 1st September

I hardly ever see my local GP but today is an exception. I have self-diagnosed what is commonly called 'a pile' up my arse.

My doctor, Bunny, is a short dumpy ginger haired Scot. She has a notoriously short temper and, as is her way, she uses much of the time allocated to tell me about her recent holiday, her forthcoming holiday and her property in Switzerland, at the same time as she painstakingly unwraps a flat box sitting on her uncluttered table top. She goes on to tell me how she must take her husband away as soon as possible because he is suffering what she diagnoses as 'extreme exhaustion.' I believe her, who wouldn't suffer from extreme exhaustion living with this woman?

All this time I am becoming more and more anxious about getting this over and done with. I play along and swoon over the new cardigan as she holds it up against her chest. If I wasn't about to show her my bum hole, I would be laughing out of frustration.

"Fwart can ay doo fir ye tadai David?"

"Err… I believe I have a pile," I blurt out, "and I'm not referring to our new hall carpet," I jest.

She visibly reels back in her seat and throws her arms in the air, probably to throw humiliation into the mix of embarrassment and acute discomfort I'm feeling right now. And then comes the big sigh of deep disappointment.

"I'll need ta have a wee look", she curses, "off wi' yer pants, up on the bed and currrl up wi' yer bum facin' 'oot," she snaps.

I pull down my trousers and underwear and assume the foetal position on the bed as instructed. I am facing away from her as she cracks on the latex gloves.

Seconds feel like minutes and minutes feel like hours before she finally, and dare I say, somewhat roughly parts my clean shaven buttocks. I can hear her tut- tutting under her breath which is very disconcerting.

"Aye, a ruddy great pile," she curses, rolling her R's like only a Scot can roll them. It's no coincidence that the paper thin walls of her office barely hide any sound between the adjoining waiting rooms.

She rips off a prescription from her printer for suppositories and as I flee past the waiting audience in the corridor I hear;

"If tha' hemeroid persists come back ta' me d'ya hear? Say helooow ta Danielle wiwl ye."

Chapter 22

Life as I knew it has been put on hold, no, more like snuffed out, finished, terminated. I'm different now.

I was going to liken it to a snake shedding its skin, but actually it's completely different to that because the snake emerges identical to how it's always looked and behaved and I am emerging as a very different person altogether.

To begin with, I can taste fear now, and I'm no longer this immortal, indestructible entity anymore, I have no control over my destiny. Suddenly I'm reliant on the voice in my head which constantly reassures me and tells me not to worry. On the odd occasion, I worry that I've gone barking mad.

A new dawn, a new worry, inexplicable pain is scorching through my left leg, a pain so intense I know instinctively there is a new threat to deal with.

Danielle humours me.

"I've looked it up. Your sciatic nerve runs right through..."

I cut into her well intentioned explanation,

"Sciatica is simply another word for leg pain," I snap, "can't you see? I'm in a whole new world of pain here!"

I continue to agonise but she's having none of it.

"You should try child birth," she quips, testing the very edges of my patience.

I hate to hurt Danielle's tender feelings, but I'm not big enough to apologise. After dosing me up with anti-inflammatories, I'm left to sleep it off.

Tuesday, my leg and my lower back have played havoc with me since about two o'clock in the morning. I'm not kidding you, this is a pain like no other pain I have ever encountered. Truly I'm frightened. As if I haven't got enough to deal with having a brain tumour, the haemorrhoid in my arse, which incidentally is an agony all of its own; it could be anything and it's growing in intensity.

By Wednesday, my leg pain is under control but now it's the turn of my father who is confined to his bed with stomach pain. Dad is never ill and this is puzzling and unsettling for all of us. So we leave Mum looking after him as we go to Addenbrooke's for my mask fitting.

For reasons unknown, my sisters decide to travel separately and arrive at the hospital late and flustered. Mobile phones don't operate here and they have no way of finding us. Eventually they sit down in a busy eating area and wait. The hospital is like a city centre, teeming with people in a hurry. The odds on bumping into us would be millions to one.

But after a couple of minutes, a man dressed in a dark suit peels away from the throng of people using the main thoroughfare of the hospital and walks straight up to them.

"I recognise you," he begins "how's your brother?"

Rachael and Louise look at one another, faintly embarrassed and definitely confused. Rachael suddenly gets it,

"Adam!" she cries, "Head of Marketing."

"Alistair," he politely corrects her and sits down to listen to their plight.

"I know exactly where you need to be," he tells them, standing up and waving his arm forward like a charge into battle. They hurriedly follow his lead through the metropolis called Addenbrooke's, through the hustle and bustle of narrow corridors, climbing up and down various stairways until finally they get to where we are waiting. Alistair vanishes before the girls can thank him properly. Apparently he did exactly the same thing when he came across my sisters coming out of the critical care ward when my life was teetering on a knife's edge. Weird.

Chapter 23

Once inside the bright white room, we soon realise the making of a mask is a highly specialised art, a bit like making a papier maché mould, but instead of newspaper, warm strips of bandage dipped in fast setting plaster are used. The eventual fit and the quality of the final Perspex finish are somewhat important. I am having a particularly powerful treatment known as stereotactic radiotherapy and if there's any movement in the mask, my brain gets frazzled.

"Nothing to worry about David, just relax if you can," Andrew, one of the two white coated technicians, tells me.

Sounds a doddle but I'm a bit claustrophobic, no problem in a small helicopter cockpit, but don't put me in the back of a two door car because I go mental.

Today I am delighted to report I have no such problems but when the last pieces are placed over my eyes I become quite emotional. I have no idea what sets me off, maybe a little self-pity creeps in, but in the darkness I'm having a good old sob.

As we all file out of the room, Andrew holds my hand.

"Remember Dave, this is just another important step in your recovery."

When we get back home, details of my six week treatment schedule are waiting for me in the post, proving this is not a dream, it's a reality. Bugger.

As we are getting ready for bed Mum calls. Dad is feeling much worse so she's called the paramedics who have arranged for him to be admitted to hospital for tests. With so much going on, the last thing we need right now is any more illness in the camp and I refuse to consider any possibility that Dad may have a problem.

Friday, and I'm taken to Addenbrooke's for an MRI scan. All my family come along just in case I kick off inside the machine.

Once inside the suffocating machine, I screw my eyes together as tightly as I can and pretend to be somewhere else. I use my fear as a tool to open my anger box and all my concentration is on the tumour. I hold nothing back, warning the tumour that I will stay in this machine for as long as it takes to get a clear shot. And I mean it.

I must have drifted off to sleep for a few minutes, suddenly, there is a jolt of the table beneath me, it's all over, and I glide out into the brightness of the room.

'One small step for David, one giant step for his confidence…'

A few days pass by before we get the call to confirm the mask is ready and an appointment has been made to fit the thing. We all feel a sense of excitement, strange as it sounds, perhaps it is the prospect of being ready to start the treatment and to start my journey of recovery.

A stern-faced nurse is waiting for me at reception when we arrive at Addenbrooke's.

"Mr Sutton?" She asks me.

This morning we are seven, the nurse is wide-eyed with surprise when all seven of us stand up together.

"Only two can come in," she protests, but we all stampede past her into the room.

The fitting process is a bit grim but the two technicians are caring and gentle. The mask covers my face and neck like a thick plastic skin, I have to fight against panicking in the most awful way, actually I can't tolerate the suffocating sensation while wearing the thing, and I plead for it to be taken off.

Now I have a problem. The sense of panic comes to me in waves, uninvited and uncontrollable. Without a mask, there will be no treatment. I have to overcome this.

I perch on one side of the table, my shoulders hunched over in despair, I have no idea how to deal with this problem. Here I am in a hospital full of sick people, some with bright yellow skin, others without any colour at all, all with miserable expressionless faces, and now I look like one of them. How did I get in such a mess? Mr super fit and healthy diet himself? Maybe this is the only way to stop me in my tracks and shake me down.

So, I need to pull myself together. I am not a loser, Hugh assures me God has a good plan for me, not a bad one, and that God is continuously testing me.

I clear my mind and listen to the voices in the room, encouraging me and reassuring me, I straighten up my back and get ready to try again.

Chapter 24

Treatment is set to begin in about ten days' time, so this weekend we are staying with my parents in Thornham, a sleepy village on the Suffolk coast. It's only half an hour away and we always love to run the dogs on the beach, and we swill down fresh mussels with real ale in ye 'ol smugglers inn.

As soon as we get to 'The Park', Mum and Dad are waiting for us and we all wander down towards the beach. The air is fresh and it takes less than ten minutes before we are crossing the marsh where tethered fishing boats are leaning at rakish angles waiting for a new tide.

Struggling for breath and with our leg muscles protesting, we climb up the Marram covered sand dunes and see the vast floor of the sea, still dark from the last tide. Charlie and Fudge sprint ahead towards the sea in the far distance, when we eventually catch up, they are happily swimming in circles of pleasure.

By the time we get back to the house, we are all exhausted and yet exhilarated by the sea air. The girls hardly have the energy to eat the meal Mum has insisted on cooking and by early evening we climb the creaking staircase and tuck our daughters into their unfamiliar beds.

What a beautiful day. If I were to be asked to describe a beautiful day just a few short weeks ago, not many of today's ingredients would have appeared on the list. It's just as if I have a new life now, and it's really mellow and comforting.

Danielle and I fall into bed and hug one another like there's no tomorrow. Neither of us utters a word, both our bodies begin to judder as we try to fight back the tears. Finally, we compose ourselves and begin to talk in whispers so as not to wake the children.

"Danielle, I'm a survivor."

"I know you are," she splutters, turning her body away and taking a bunch of tissues from the bedside table.

She sits up in the bed and holds a tissue up to her nose. As she blows, the silence of night is rudely broken, it's a deafening sound like a trumpet to my ear and both of us, spontaneously and uncontrollably burst into laughter.

And it's enough to wake Emily in the next-door bedroom, so I go and settle her. Moments later she is fast asleep again, clutching at my hand against her soft cheek. A shaft of light from the landing light cuts diagonally across her bed and I can see her long eyelashes and her gorgeous pouting lips, slightly parted as she draws each long breath. I don't want to move. I feel a tear slide down my cheek, I want so much for Emily and Hannah to be proud of their father. Why has it taken all of this to wake me up and realise how lucky I am?

Chapter 25

I am a couple of days away from starting my treatment for a brain tumour. Disbelief constantly circles my thoughts, I still harbour a crazy suspicion that I am in some sort of nightmare and I constantly have to fan the flames of hope by remembering that treatment heralds the beginning of my recovery.

I keep myself busy answering e-mails and showing estate agents around our house. Now the business has crashed we are relying on Danielle's salary and some property rental. But our mortgages are something like seven grand a month so this isn't enough. Unless something pretty miraculous happens, we'll be broke in a matter of weeks.

We are not surprised, but still disappointed to hear the house is worth less than we hoped, a lot less actually, around £600,000 shy of a valuation given just a couple of years ago, "And the market is falling all the time," today's agent tells us, sucking his teeth and trying his best to look sympathetic.

We don't plan to discuss this news with our building society any time soon.

I cannot understand why I am so unfazed about everything, the business crashing, my tumour, our financial crisis. My conversations with Hugh have encouraged me to pray, a lot. When I do, the voice in my head always reassures me, and I'm pretty sure these reassurances are responsible for my positive and calm sense of mind. There's no other explanation.

Chapter 26

In between all the disbelief and the shock, moments of normal life break through, and today, it's in the form of Dad's determination to clear up the disgusting mess the Administrators left behind and to raise some much-needed cash.

Today's objective is to turn all the old machinery and scrap metal scattered around the site into money. Amazing how much crap the business has accumulated over the past few years, but by mid-afternoon an ageing lorry trundles unsteadily out of the yard laden with a mountainous pile of assorted jagged metals bound for the local scrap yard.

"Good work boys," dad says rubbing his hands together, "I wouldn't be surprised if there's a couple of thousand quid there."

It's great to see dad a bit more like his normal, happy and optimistic self again, away from the stress of losing the business and the deeper stress of my health problems.

Hugh and I are not so confident, £1000 would be a victory we tell him. Mind you, what do we know about scrap metal?

We hang around in the empty offices for an hour or so waiting for the call. When it comes, even I am surprised. £100.

"Every little helps," Dad sighs as he wearily climbs into his car and heads back on the coast road to Thornham.

What a character he is, I hope I'm like him when I'm 80.

Chapter 27

Saturday is the designated day to book a summer holiday overseas and to spend the weekend in Thornham with mum and dad. I smugly predict a deal of the century, after all this country is in the worst recession in living memory and the value of the euro makes everywhere in Europe incredibly expensive, so there must be bags of availability at knockdown prices. We plump for a luxury hotel in Le Touquet, travelling by train, I have in mind a penthouse suite.

My ill-judged confidence and, dare I say, the almost arrogant tone to my voice is met with far greater authority from French hoteliers, all of whom scoff at the notion of available rooms in this resort at this time of year.

By the end of the day, I have spoken to all the French hotels who are prepared to speak in English and also to every five star hotel between Norwich and Cornwall. I make so many calls that my throat is hoarse and I've lost my voice.

Never one to be beaten, I have a cunning plan up my sleeve which I'm hoping Danielle and the girls will go for.

Chapter 28

In the evening, we wander down the narrow street from The Park to the local Gastro pub, now famed for its pizzas rather than its smugglers. All of the wider family are here, grandparents, grandchildren, parents, sons, daughters, in-laws, the whole shebang.

Once inside I recognise several familiar faces and I notice how each and every one of them smiles awkwardly as I thread my way through to the small stone-walled room we have reserved. Bad news travels fast I suppose, but if anybody is looking for any signs of fear or defeat, they will be very disappointed. There will be people in the pub who, in the past, have judged me as a heartless playboy. It's a small community and I can take a sneer or two because my reputation for fast living must have pissed a few people off. The truth is I feel no self-pity because the little voice in my head keeps telling me I'm going to get through this and come out the other side a much better person.

In the flickering candlelight, we all sit around the long wooden table in the centre of the room and spend the evening eating good food and drinking even better wine, and the short walk back along the empty village Street is a perfect end to a great evening together.

During the night, tender little Hannah is up with a high temperature and a stomach upset. I am fully aware that both she and Emily are confused and worried that I'm in and out of hospital, and it's vital for me to reassure them that everything will be okay. Nothing hurts me more than to see my children worrying like this. By morning, she is back to her normal, chipper self, declaring I am her saviour!

Early in the morning we are woken by the thud of the front door slamming. The girls race into our bedroom to ask what the noise is and we open the curtains to look outside. Hugh is taking off in his car, spinning his wheels in the gravel. Mum is running behind him in hot pursuit. She has her arm held high and is waving what looks like a wad of cash in the air.

To witness their elderly grandmother dressed only in a raspberry and gold dressing gown chasing Hugh's car up the driveway has the girls hooting with laughter,

"Is Gran okay?" asks Emily with a puzzled look on her face.

"No," I tell her, "she's barking mad."

The girls squeal with delight and disbelief when she staggers back into the house, panting like a dog and laughing at her own crazy ways.

After breakfast, at Hugh's suggestion, we drive along the narrowing coastal road to Walsingham Abbey, otherwise known as 'Our Lady of Walsingham' and named after Mary, mother of Jesus, who appeared here as an apparition in 1061.

Apparently, pilgrims travel from all over the world to take the healing waters which are drawn from the Abbey's famous well.

Our plan is to take some healing water and hopefully receive a blessing. I do feel a sense of shame and embarrassment because I've always been too busy having fun to pay any attention to God. I must look a bit of a fraud through his eyes I suppose.

After 20 minutes or so, we come to a flintstone pub called The Victoria which boasts a great reputation for real ale and traditional Sunday lunches. Today's visit turns out to be a double whammy when we see a giant buttercup-yellow rescue helicopter parked majestically in the empty meadow beside the pub.

Hannah shares my passion for helicopters and once inside the pub we head straight for the crew, dressed in their olive green overalls. They've popped in for a spot of lunch, as one does. After I was kicked out of public school, I went straight on to have an interview with the Royal Navy to fly helicopters. I think the phrase they used at the time was 'not what we're looking for at the moment'.

Sensing our passion, the crew invite us to look around the awesome machine as it crouches on the pale yellow grass.

We listen wide-eyed to the first-hand accounts of many rescues the helicopter and its crew have been involved with, and we all get a sense of how brave and capable these individuals are.

Feeling the aircraft on the outside and taking in all the different textures and scents on the inside reminds me of why I yearned to become one of these magnificent men in their flying machine.

We are blown away by their impeccable hospitality and when it's time for them to go, we stand cocooned within the excitement of the deafening roar of the jet engines and the swirling air around us as the powerful rotors begin to thump their way through the warm air.

Amid the roar of the powerful jet engines, I glance over to see the expressions on Hannah and Emily's faces, their eyes narrowed into the brightness of the day, waving their arms furiously and jumping up and down with excitement, I know this moment will always be etched in their memories. It will be etched in mine too, that's for certain.

Stepping inside the Abbey there is definitely a sense of reverence, a feeling that this is a special place. A special healing service is about to begin and we all join in, standing at the back of the small church. Mum, Dad, Hugh, Louise, Rachael, Danielle and I, all find ourselves in tears at one point or another, Emily and Hannah are straight-faced. We all take our place in the queue to receive a blessing and when they are asked whether they have any particular need, they both asked quietly for 'God to make Daddy better please'. It breaks my heart.

We travel back home after a great weekend in Thornham, it's obvious to me that my diagnosis has affected everybody, some more than others, but I have noticed the subtle changes.

Later in the evening back at home, I take Charlie and Fudge out for a walk, along the front lawn up to the Meadow where sheep close their eyes beneath a sky splattered with twinkling stars and where the aroma of dry grass tingles my nostrils. The dogs sniff, pee and shit as is their bedtime routine, whilst I simply take in the fresh, still air. Alone, leaning on the metal gate, I close my eyes and start talking,

"God or Jesus, if you're listening, I want to say thank you. I realise you've had your work cut out looking after me, and to be fair, I've never really appreciated all the times you've had to step in to protect me. But everything has changed now, I'll prove it, and if you can give me the time to raise Emily and Hannah and long enough for me to get to know their children, I'll be happy to move up with you. I'd appreciate it if you could forgive me for leading such a pointless life so far, I promise I'll make you proud of me if I have more time. The doctors have written me off, you know I'm shit scared underneath, but I think the voices in my head come from you, and you're telling me everything will be alright. If it is you, I can't thank you enough. Please please please can I have a second chance?"

Chapter 29

I keep finding myself going over and over everything that's happened to me in such a small space of time. It's a chilling sequence of bizarre and most terrible events that have changed all of our lives. At least it can't get any worse. Anyway, it goes a bit like this:

1. Out of the blue, with no warning, I've been robbed of my livelihood and much of the wealth I built up in the business over 20 ball breaking years, everything, snatched away from me in an instant.

2. Again, quite out of the blue, and with no warning, I've been viciously attacked, head butted in a particular spot on my face which triggered a series of events that resulted in the detection of a brain tumour.

3. I've managed to tolerate a toxic cocktail of chemicals which kept me alive on the life support machine; not everyone is so lucky.

4. Eminent surgeons tell me I have weeks to live.

5. I am about to start radiotherapy on my brain and a course of chemotherapy which contains the most toxic chemicals a human being can withstand.

6. Doctors tell me I'm only here at all because of the exceptional condition of my liver, my heart and lungs, so

I find it weird that six months ago I gave up alcohol and as a result my liver is clean as a new pin.

It's double weird that about the same time that I banned alcohol from my system, I also upped my fitness regime and running program, enhancing the function and capability of my heart and lungs. Was all of this preparing me for what lay ahead? Because I had no real reason to do any of these things.

Because of all this strangeness, I'm being seduced by the heady notion that someone or something is looking after me, that the voice I hear when I pray, and the feelings of falling in love with Jesus might actually be real.

Chapter 30

"What's it like when you die?" asks Emily, and Hannah follows up with part two of their query,

"Does it hurt?"

With those awkward questions still ringing in my ears, I start the first of thirty daily train journeys back and forth to hospital.

For the first couple of weeks, I keep my energy levels pretty high, jogging along the farm tracks and around the apple orchards that surround our house. It's the best feeling to take in the clean air and hold my face up to the sun.

My old way of life is fading away, fast. Calls from friends and colleagues wanting to know the scary details have dried up. It doesn't surprise me nor does it worry me, in fact it pleases me, only my closest family members matter to me now, I'm happy to be cocooned inside a new world, in which the only currency is love.

I prefer not to have visitors, their feigned sympathies and empty gestures are easy to spot, I simply use my time focusing on getting better.

There are exceptions of course, like when brother-in-law Bruce turns up with Pastor Okafor, a stranger who he met by chance and who was 'waiting for someone or something to call on him'.

He is from Nigeria, visiting England on a mission to find second-hand goods for his parishioners back home.

In my opinion, Nigeria has more than its fair share of scallywags, but I take him at face value. He is easy to talk to, he listens very closely to everything I have to say and he flicks through pages of the Bible with consummate ease, back and forth, reading out loud the relative verses, eloquently and with a clear understanding,

"Glory be to God, you will be healed," are his final words. I like him and I hope our paths will cross in the future.

Chapter 31

Radiotherapy is a very precise art. Zap the wrong bit and you can be left a gibbering idiot, or worse. Sarah tells me how meticulous she has been in programming my treatment, even taking into account how precious I am about my hair. At the time, I was nonplussed, I just wanted to be saved, hair or no hair.

Today, Saturday, is haircut day. Sarah warned me that I will lose much of my hair for a while and recently I have been pulling the stuff out in clumps.

Armed with my new barber's kit, Hugh has offered to execute the number one.

Emily and Hannah have always seen me with long hair and a ponytail. Once or twice I wore dreadlocks, loved them, I've bleached it white and dyed it red, don't want them to see this as something bad or negative, I need it to be fun.

Hugh has all of us laughing from the off, Emily and Hannah look on, doing their best to join in the fun, but at the same time they are beginning to realise this is not a game.

Still in shock with my new bald look, they scream with laughter as Hugh insists on shaving his own head in solidarity. His own hair is curly and very dense and the girls bag it up and take it outside for birds to make nests.

Sunday, and I feel dog tired after a bad night's sleep. Some time ago we agreed to do a sponsored walk in aid of the Brain Tumour Trust. Today is the day and I make heavy work of it and by the time we finish I'm virtually sleep walking.

Hannah is unwell in the night, in my past life I would have nudged Danielle in the ribs and let her get on with it, but now, despite my exhaustion, it's my privilege to climb into her bed, stroke her soft skin and take hold of her small hand. Each time she wakes I kiss her on the cheek or on her soft neck, and she slides back into another shallow sleep. Hannah and Emily are such tender souls, all I want now is enough time to see both of them love their own children with the same depth and intensity I feel at this moment.

Monday is marred by a fainting episode in the kitchen. It frightens all of us, the paramedics are summoned. I am learning very quickly that doctors, surgeons, specialists, nurses and paramedics, often can't say for any real certainty why things happen. After the usual checks, both of the serious eyed medics dressed in their bright green overalls give me the all clear but with the option to go to hospital, which I gracefully decline.

The next day, as the train click-clacks into Cambridge station, I feel another fainting episode coming on. It's scary because all sorts of things go through my mind, I wonder if I am about to die.

More and more these days, I am praying and listening to the voice in my head, 'am I dying? Am I dying?' I semi-panic, 'please save me' I beg, and the reply is steadfast, 'all part of your recovery' comes straight back.

We spill out of the busy train, Hugh holds me as I stumble across the platform and collapse on a bench seat. Now I'm shit-scared, yet at the same time I believe the little voice in my head telling me this will pass.

Commuters crane their necks as they bustle along the platform, hoping to catch a glimpse of the poor bugger crying on the bench, my family do their best to shield me and Danielle calls for the ambulance. Again.

Another bone-rattling journey to hospital (there's a market for an ambulance that handles well and doesn't rattle) and I'm checked into Addenbrooke's for an overnight stay, 'just for observation'.

Chapter 32

My ward is sprinkled with seven ghostly looking old men. This is a cancer ward.

The first thing I notice is the strange odour in here, it's like disinfectant masking the stronger odour of shit, maybe some vomit in there as well. The air is rancid, so much so that I try not to breathe through my nose.

The fainting episode has passed now and I cast my eyes over my fellow inmates. There are seven others, I don't know it yet, but by morning the tally will be down to five.

The first to go is a man in his mid-60s I guess. He is wearing a thin, silky dressing gown and an ill-fitting wig. I name him Wiggie due to his ill-fitting hair piece.

I watch him pace up and down the ward but he avoids any eye contact just like all the other poor critters in here.

I am dozing when I hear the screech of a bedside alarm sounding at the far end of the ward. It's 'Wiggie', mostly obscured by a curtain. A nurse hurries in and as she makes her way down the ward she is swishing as many curtains across as she can. When she reaches his bed, there's more frantic swishing until he is finally sealed away from view. By now, he is screaming at the top of his voice, a deep, agonising tone which is fucking terrible to listen to. The alarm is turned off and **now**, without the metallic sound of curtains being drawn, there are one or two seconds of silence before the wretched sound of liquid matter splashing against the plastic floor, takes over and fills the room. More pitiful cries ring out, and then a much louder alarm begins to sound, this time with far greater urgency, and within seconds, I hear the hurried footsteps of lifesavers, I hope, bursting into the ward and running to the man's bed.

All of us listen to the frantic, competing voices as they battle to save a man's life, it's scary, then the whole show races back through the ward and out into the main corridor.

The carnival of gabbling voices gradually disappears from earshot as the bed speeds through the hospital, and as quickly as this terrible episode has started, it's all over, only the bloody footprints on the plastic floor give any hint of the man's battle for life.

Most people would describe this place as hell on earth. I simply have no words to convey what it feels like to be here. It's shocking, I want to run away, but what would that achieve asks the voice in my head. I have no option but to stand and fight and meet this thing head on. I put my hands together and pray.

Chapter 33

Each and every second feels like time on another planet, impossible to gauge and inconsequential, time is fucked, my existence is in the balance and I'm halfway to hell. Each time I get out of bed to visit the bathroom, I try to engage with the other lepers in the colony. I want to help them but don't know how, one or two are too ill to acknowledge me, others try to talk in crackling voices.

The eldest looking one of the bunch, a tall ancient looking man, reluctantly nods back to me as I pass his bed en-route to the khazi. I'm very aware that, in this ward, I need to choose my words carefully.

"Hi, my name's David Sutton," I tell him taking hold of his long, thin fingers which stay motionless on top of his bed covers, "and I'll be your captain today."

I'm sure there's a flicker of a smile in his eyes,

"John," he croaks.

"What's the deal with visiting hours here John?"

"Next session, seven p.m.," he whispers knowingly.

Underneath the growl of his voice box I can hear a military type accent to match his silver, closely cropped hair and moustache. He is, or was, a distinguished gentleman.

"Who'll come tonight then?" I ask, hoping the reply is 'the wife' or 'my daughter', anybody he is close to and who will cheer him up. His empty expression looks to me like he's run out of energy and lost the will to fight, and he must feel so lonely in this hell hole,

"I won't let them see me like this," he says in a tone full of pride.

I am not sure what I should say next, so I just tell it as it comes.

"For me, it's my family that keep me together, I don't know what I would have done without them. And my faith."

I'm so comfortable telling him this, it's crystal clear to me at this moment that I know the little voice in my head is real, God is real, Jesus is real, my prayers are being answered and the miracles that continuously save me, are real.

John maintains his empty expression, I sense all of this is going over his head, but he levels his eyes up to my own,

"I've had throat cancer and now prostate cancer," is all he says before closing his eyes. I don't know whether he hears me or not, but I tell him I will pray for him.

I walk away back up the ward and stop by the bed opposite my own. This time, the guy holds his arm up to say hello.

We chat, much in the same vein as I did with John, only Brian is far more interested in the faith vibe. By the time I climb back into my own bed, I am sort of feeling good about myself.

Chapter 34

I must have drifted off to sleep because when I wake up I see the smiling face of Pastor Okafor who is standing at the end of my bed alongside a tall elegant woman he introduces as Veronica, his wife. It's a big surprise, I am slightly embarrassed but I'm very pleased to see him again. There are other visitors dotted around the ward, none beside John, and I figure it must be seven in the evening.

They have travelled all the way from Liverpool to see me before they go back to Nigeria. For a long time we chat together, I'm impressed with their in-depth knowledge of biblical times and listening to both of them is uplifting and inspiring. Pastor O plans to sleep on the floor beside my bed but the nurses will have none of it. He is clearly offended and I find this experience very humbling. How many of my buddies or colleagues would do this? How many of them, with no transport of their own, and at great personal expense, would willingly endure the seven hour rail journey, having to change trains and take taxis in a country they don't know, just to sit beside me and reassure me?

The number is less than one.

I try to tell him that I don't deserve their kindness but he is adamant and happy because he realises that I am the purpose of his trip to England. He considers himself as a messenger to tell me the good news.

Before they are forced to leave, Pastor O stands next to my bed and talks to me in a firm tone of voice, assuring me I am cured and that God has a purpose for me. The three of us pray together before he and Veronica walk out of the ward, slowly and majestically, smiling and nodding to patients either side of the ward. They remind me of a Zulu king and queen, their gracious, statesmanlike body language is enough to raise a feeble hand or two as they pass through. Wow. Thank you Jesus.

Chapter 35

Secretly I dread the thought of lying awake through the night, having to listen to a chorus of shallow musical lungs straining on the inhale and increasingly shallow on the exhale, but after the visitors leave, a team of two nurses dressed in white push a small drugs trolley through the ward, dishing out various potions to each patient. I am offered sleeping tablets which I gladly take under the watchful eye of matron.

Mercifully, I am for the main part under sedation, asleep yet vaguely conscious of movement around me, like when I hear the faint squeak of bed wheels gliding through the ward. It's all a bit surreal, like when I smoked heroin from the surface of a piece of silver paper many years ago. I must have been crazy, but in those days nothing fazed me, I was indestructible, immortal, and I wanted to experience everything life had to throw at me.

Dawn emerges from a blue-black hue, when the neon lights flicker into life I shield my eyes away from the stark brightness, I'm very groggy but I notice a figure standing beside Brian's bed.

I doze off and when I come around again I glance along the ward. There are two empty bed spaces now, one was Wiggie's, the other where an old and frail man took his last breath. They're dropping like flies.

Opposite me, Brian's wife, I presume, perches straight-backed on the seat beside his bed. She oozes dignity and is holding Brian's hand and chatting incessantly. She turns her head to look at me and throws a generous smile, then suddenly gets up from her seat and walks to the end of my bed.

"I've come to pick up Brian," she begins. I don't know whether this is a good thing or a bad thing but she's still smiling,

"Thank you David." She continues.

I'm puzzled, but she quickly moves on, "you really cheered Brian up last night," she tells me in a half whisper. 'Get well soon' is her parting message.

She wastes no time in gathering up his things, dressing him and moving out. They leave me filled with a sense of satisfaction, of pure pleasure at having made a difference to somebody when it really counted.

On my way to the bathroom once again, still heady from praise, I pass by two nurses struggling to strap John into some form of harness in order to lift him off his bed.

"I've lost the use of my legs!" he calls out to me despairingly. He is looking directly at me as if to say, 'I'd rather be dead than humiliated like this, you understand what I'm saying don't you David?'

This is the last time I will see John Evans.

Chapter 36

I am home. Thank you God or Jesus or whoever I have to thank for rescuing me from that hellhole.

I am very weak, not like me at all, and I've lost confidence in myself for the first time in my life, I'm a wreck, and it frightens me.

For the next few days, I travel back and forth to Addenbrooke's for more blood tests. These tests will determine whether or not I continue with treatment. If my body can't tolerate the radiotherapy or chemotherapy, well, I don't know what happens.

All my family look so washed out, Emily and Hannah walk around with unsmiling expressions on their faces, and I feel powerless to help them.

Chapter 37

My bloods come out okay so we're back in business. By the weekend, I am well and truly knackered, mostly from the radiotherapy but the chemo is taking its toll now.

Saturday evening, I have enough energy to creep downstairs, slowly step by step, but progress comes to an abrupt halt as a wave of panic smothers my mind and leaves me semiconscious before Danielle calls the paramedics in. Again.

We go through the same routine; me lying on the floor, Emily and Hannah ushered into another room, Danielle explaining all the grisly details of my prognosis and my treatment, paramedics shaking their heads, not knowing what the answer is or indeed what the question is, whether the treatment or the tumour is the catalyst here.

The ambulance arrives, I'm put onto a stretcher, loaded up and we're off to the Accident and Emergency department. AGAIN. Mum and Dad, brother Hugh and my sisters join Danielle and they all gather around me.

I guess this is even more stressful for them than it is for me, because all of this time I am praying for help and the little voice in my head is telling me everything will be okay. And I believe it.

It is four o'clock in the morning before I finally pass the medical checks and go home.

On Sunday, my confidence drops to an all-time low. I lie rigid on my bed terrified that I will trigger another episode. I loathe myself for being so fucking feeble and so frightened, in the afternoon I pluck up the courage and strength to climb out of bed and hobble downstairs. I pick at a cooked chicken from the refrigerator and drink some cold water, all the time just waiting for another 'episode' to come and take me down again. I am so lucky to have my family around but I feel like I'm in a bubble, sort of detached from the rest of the world.

Back in my bedroom I catch a glimpse of the day through the tall Georgian windows. It's a bright squally day and I narrow my eyes to scan our front garden to where the yellow-green leaves of a giant beech tree are being torn horizontally from their branches by fierce gusts of a northern wind. They skip and bounce into the tall grass. The wind subsides and the following gust begins to gather momentum.

My sister Rachael drives an electric car, it glides into vision, breaking my vacant gaze and brings me back to my senses. From above, I watch her walk into the kitchen and a couple of minutes later she comes out with Emily and Hannah. Now I remember, she made a promise to take them shopping for water colour paint brushes and drawing paper, something to distract the girls away from the stress and worry enveloping the house, and here she is making good on that promise. My only regret is that today I'm left behind, gazing into the middle distance, too tired to wave let alone attempt such a feat. How my life has changed.

Chapter 38

A bright Monday morning heralds the beginning of a new week of treatment. As we make our way to Cambridge, I stare out of the car window with my eyes blinded with the low autumn sun. The road runs some twenty or thirty meters above ground level, and I can see in the far distance of the flat, fen landscape, field after field dissected into irregular sizes and shapes by a labyrinth of dykes and thorn hedgerows dotted in bright red with their winter berries.

I lean my weary head against the side window to cool the embers of my scorched brain, my eyes are closed but I can still make out the passing shadows of tall trees and shafts of bright sunlight in between.

When I do force my eyelids open, I can see green-black water in a river down below; its surface shimmers in white as rolling winds pass over at speed. As I take in all of this natural beauty surrounding me, I can feel regret and disappointment gnawing away at the edges of my mind because I have never stopped to appreciate these simple pleasures. I have pretty much taken everything for granted.

If I get a second chance at life, I will never take anything for granted, ever again.

And so begins the first of this week's radiotherapy sessions, of lying down on the cold surface of the machine, of having the claustrophobic mask clamped tightly over my face and finally of the deep sense of elation I feel as each session comes to an end.

That sense of elation and my faith in God is all that keeps me from freaking out, ripping my head out from the mask and running as far away as I can.

I've worked out that the reassuring and calming voice inside of me has to be Jesus tuning in. I couldn't make up the simple but powerful messages that come through, and in all honesty, I couldn't do this without him.

The week goes by in a haze of repetition, travel to Cambridge, get zapped, travel back home and spend the rest of the day in a semiconscious state before climbing back into bed in the early evening.

And the little voice in my head tells me over and over again, this is all part of recovery...

Chapter 39

Can leopards change their spots? Probably not, but in the case of us mortal human beings, I'm sure we can. I have. Often, in the middle of black, blustery nights I am talking to God. The pleasure I got from the heartfelt thanks Brian's wife gave me can't be valued in terms of money and has infinitely more value than any possession.

Chapter 40

If you take an aerial view of our tiny slice of the English countryside, you will see a Georgian farm house, not a stately home by any stretch of the imagination but still a pretty large house by normal standards, surrounded by acres of grassy paddocks with giant trees, beech, oak and elm. All framed in dense woodland.

Two or three years ago, I can't remember exactly when, but each time I finished my cross country runs, I got into the habit of resting beneath the canopy of a giant oak tree which stands in the middle of the meadow facing our house.

There I would air all of my woes, feel all the negatives and often complain. What a fool I've been.

Chapter 41

Yeeha! I'm halfway through my radiotherapy. A kind-eyed African nurse called Tchebe explains how the therapy will be ramped up from this point using a narrower focus, 'onto where the little bugger was'. His small and surely deliberate use of the past tense fills me with pleasure.

I like him, he takes particular care removing my gold watch, necklace and crucifix and we chat about our shared faith before I lie down for my radiotherapy session.

Today's session passes quickly, I am calm and walk out of the room to see an elderly woman next in the queue with two teenage boys, one on either side of her, grandchildren I guess, all looking a bit glum,

"It's a doddle," I tell her in a cheery voice, "and remember, this is all part of your recovery."

"Thank you dear," she chirps up, clearly surprised,

"I'll think about that when I'm in there," she smiles.

Oh how I like being a nice guy, I begin loitering in the waiting room after treatment to spot the weaker patients in need of a pep talk. Today I notice Danielle hanging back to talk with an old guy who I talked to earlier. She catches up with me in the corridor, she tells me the man was saying a big thank you to me for raising the spirits of his wife recently, "she really needed it," he told Danielle. Oh how I like being a nice guy.

This evening, lying with Danielle in our giant four-poster bed watching television, I'm in a philosophical mood,

"How would you describe me Danielle?" I ask. She stays silent, glued to her favourite period drama. She sighs, loudly.

"How do you mean?" she asks in a somewhat disinterested tone of voice, not bothering to turn her head away from the TV.

"Well, if you were asked to describe who I am in less than 20 words, what words would you use?"

She starts fumbling around the crumpled bed sheets to find the remote controls, if I'm not mistaken, there's a hint of impatience in the air. Another louder sigh comes before her patience wears thin.

"Darling, you know I love this, it's only got another five minutes, can this wait?"

"Nope," I joke. She fumbles beneath the sheets with the maximum of fuss and bother, finds the handset and puts the favourite program on hold.

"I vill say zis only vonce," she jests "because a Jeremy Paxman interview is starting in eight minutes and I need to finish this."

I'm listening, genuinely wondering what she's about to say, Danielle has a knack of being one step ahead of me. After a short pause for thought, she begins,

"You're a marketing genius (I take this seriously) and a talented writer (ditto)."

There is a pause, I wait patiently for the longer list of accolades to keep coming, but her blank expression gives

111

the game away so I switch the bedside lights off and turn to face her.

"What are you looking at me like that for?" she asks. I'm fishing for compliments here and she knows it.

"I'm thinking you might have one or two more positives maybe?"

Her most dramatic, loudest sigh of the evening is followed by this;

"Well okay, if you insist. Let's see. In fairness, you hardly ever fart.

Danielle is s straight faced and as we look into one another's eyes, I get a sense of the anguish and hurt she's going through and I want to make her smile, "If I cut the farting out, you stop picking your nose. Deal?"

When Danielle calms down and catches her breath, she turns to face me, draping one arm over my shoulder and looking deep into my eyes.

"Te amo, I've loved you from the moment we met in the women's toilets (it's a long story) all those years ago." I giggle and she picks up her conversation again, "I love you for who you really are, a kind-hearted, gentle, loving person. Success changed you David, and not for the better I might add," she says wryly, "you've shed that skin now."

A thoughtful pause hovers between us,

"Now shut up and let me get back to my program," she jokes.

We both cackle away, as if we haven't a care in the world. Thank God I've got Danielle.

Chapter 42

Today I lose track of time. I guess it's a Wednesday, and with pencil and paper to hand, I'm in what I would describe as a reflective mood. I feel the need to take a mental stock of all the bizarre events that have turned my life upside down over the last few months. Maybe if I piece them all together again, I will find some answers.

1. Our business partner deceived and betrayed us, the carnage he left behind almost destroyed us, spiritually and financially. What sort of crook is he to want to inflict such pain upon a family who has been so good to him?

2. The flip side to this question is that by doing so, we have been freed from the shackles of a life that bought very little happiness or contentment for Hugh or myself. Plenty of money but no fun. Does this mean, in some obscure way, I should be grateful to this moron?

3. Should I be grateful to the thug who assaulted me, for the cowardly way he smashed his forehead into my face with such force that it nearly killed me?

4. Thank you Jesus for the bizarre and the unpredictable.

5. Was it just good luck that I discovered Professor Prada? His miraculous rejection of my prognosis, against all the odds, and in contrast to what I had been told by

other experts, convinced me to believe the voice in my head was real, and I was going to survive and recover from all of this.

6. Before the assault, I had no symptoms of any brain tumour whatsoever. Very often, brain tumours make their presence known only when it's too late to treat them. If I hadn't been assaulted, in the way I was, it could have struck when I was driving my family or when I was at the controls of a helicopter. I was due to take my first solo flight around Norwich airport shortly after I was attacked. Is all of this just coincidence?

Chapter 43

I don't believe in coincidence. If I wasn't convinced before all of this, I'm convinced now that somebody out there is taking care of me. I know for certain, after all that's happened recently, there is a greater force at work, a creator, I call him God. I believe he has a son too, called Jesus. I get the whole gig, it makes sense to me.

My antenna is tuned into a totally different frequency now, and just as I have always wanted to please my dad, I feel an even stronger desire to please God. I write to the self-proclaimed president of Zimbabwe, President Mugabe, to remind him that even he could receive forgiveness if he turned to God. I tell him God offers his love. Unsurprisingly I get no reply from his office.

I write to General Laurent Nkunda, another monster masquerading as a freedom fighter using children as young as nine years old to carry out unspeakable atrocities. I write to him offering God's love, urging him to stop and seek forgiveness. No reply.

On my daily trips to Addenbrooke's, I take hand written quotes from the Bible to give to others facing the zapper.

As my treatment continues, I reach new depths of fatigue, barely able to climb the stairs and undress when I get back home.

My body, my life, is slowly being crushed, but as I crawl naked over crisp white bed sheets like a stalking leopard, and lay my body against the icy cool linen, I am smiling inside because I know this is all part of my recovery.

Chapter 44

I dream. Didn't used to, but more often than not, it's a message from Jesus like, 'David you are cured', over and over again.

Last night I dreamt about a man I know well. Fred is a buyer for a supermarket chain, he played an important role in our business and at the time our partner disappeared we were totally dependent on the £12 million or so of trade generated between our respective companies.

Many years ago by a quirk of fate, Fred was promoted from the shop floor to the buying department, swapping his scruffy overalls for a suit and tie overnight.

It didn't take long for suppliers to catch on to the fact that Fred was dyslexic and totally inexperienced. While some mocked his disability, and others took advantage of his naivete, Hugh and I chose to help him. He had no product knowledge, no negotiating skills, not a clue how to do his job effectively. We held his hand, showed him the ropes, told him the truth, helped him sift through the bullshit he was being fed from other suppliers. We saved his arse time and time again.

When we first met Fred, he and his wife were Jehovah's Witnesses, knocking on doors, dedicating themselves to passing on the word of God. Fred was humble and grateful, but as time passed by his confidence grew. And grew. And grew. Soon enough he became intoxicated with the power a supermarket buyer yields, taking every perk on offer, cash, VIP trips to European Grand Prix's, fishing trips, hookers you name it. He became crazed with power, travelling around the world, often to third world countries desperate for his business.

The long-suffering wife was dropped, a new younger version was quickly recruited and two children produced, the Jehova's Witness gig was kicked into touch. From a position of integrity, as far as we were concerned, Fred became a total arse hole, corrupt, greedy, arrogant and ungrateful. Our relationship changed from one of respect, to one of fear. His favourite phrase became 'Fook 'em', whenever a supplier struggled to meet a deadline, followed by a hefty fine, often dished out on a Friday, 'to really fook their weekend up'. He became a monster.

After our business partner did a runner, unsurprisingly Fred was nowhere to be seen, he turned his back on us and moved on.

I wake up so elated I laugh out loud. Those were the bad old days.

Chapter 45

Today is Wednesday, I think, the last day of my treatment. Rock on! I take time to thank God and Jesus for getting me through, still the all-consuming fatigue pins every muscle down as I lay on the bed like a condemned man strapped down onto the execution table.

In the early evening, Dad is full of excitement at the prospect of starting a new business; storage and distribution out of our existing warehouses. I never cease to be amazed at Dad's appetite for business, here he is, eighty odd and still leading from the front. Top man.

Hugh reads to me out loud, it's a short biblical story about Job, a man who seemingly has everything, only to have it all taken away, his wealth, his family and his health. And for his unfailing loyalty and faith in God during such a devastating time, his life is restored, his wealth returned and his family and loved ones returned. As you can imagine, this strikes a chord.

Without the daily routine back and forth to Cambridge, some sort of normality creeps back into our lives. The smallest improvement heralds a growing confidence; I begin to pee standing up again, hurrah! Progress! I walk upstairs and downstairs, two times, hurrah! Progress! I manage to watch five minutes of TV without my head spinning like a top, hurrah! Progress!

Chapter 46

All the family are drained, I see it in their creased expressions, fortunately Emily and Hannah are holding up brilliantly, Danielle has stepped up to the plate, taking on all the responsibilities that until recently we shared together. She's a rock.

Last night was a long night, for some reason my body gave sleep a swerve, I catch sight of myself in the mirror, pale faced, with my eyes deep into their sockets. I tell myself, 'this is only temporary, all part of my recovery', but I can't help but realise just how wrecked I look at the moment.

But hey! I'm alive thank God.

Dreams are more and more weird. Last night I woke up and began scribbling like a fiend. It's a song, I think, and this is how it goes;

Taking time out I can finally see,
It's all been a relief actually,
It's not about booze or drugs,
Or the long legged girls,
Their G strings or their sexy ughs,
That was all about me.
Truth is, it's all about Him.

Respect him, love him, fear Him,
'Cause when you get burned, when your life turns, He's
the only one who can bring it in.

Chorus;

When I tell you, it may seem too simple but listen,
I know what it's all about now,
I'm so happy, it's so simple,
It's about Him, not you or me,
It's all about Him.

I prance back and forth on centre stage,
Throwing my creativity
Over frenzied expressions,
Like throwing hundred dollar bills,
My words spurt and froth over upturned faces,
I want to hug all of them and tell them,

Chorus

In three score years and ten, maybe a handful more,
Even I will turn to walk through heaven's door,
When I take my last look behind me and see my life's
achievements, will it make me smile with pleasure and
pride?

Chorus

Have I walked this Earth as Jesus did?
And will God be pleased with me?

I will take with me the memories
of good times, or maybe they weren't,
I'm not so sure now.

Chorus

Will my biography have any meaning?
'Cause I was so lucky,
To come off that ride before it was too late,
And my life was turned around,
And I got a second chance.

Chorus

The ageing fans and soulless friends have moved on,
I begin to use my life
For the purposes God set out, He's forgiven me for
everything,
And now it's time to shout

How I pray for the billionaires and trillionaires
Who aren't rich like me,
But I have to keep doing my thing,
Which will help set us free…

   I have no idea what these ramblings mean, one day I'll
read them and they might make some sense.

Chapter 47

My laboured breathing since the treatment began, is gradually returning to normal, hurrah!

Microscopic hair follicles are emerging from my tender scalp once again, hurrah!

Physical and mental energy is creeping back so I can catch up with my admin and texting any friends left, hurrah!

But when it boils down to it, I am left with very few worthwhile friendships. The hangers-on disappeared after the business went down, no real surprise there, but when seemingly genuine and trusted friends turn their backs, it hurts. One such example is a chap who I will call Maurice. He's knighted and he's a billionaire, someone who should be genuine, someone with integrity and decency. I've been a generous friend to him in the past. When our business partner disappeared and trouble came galloping over the horizon, I asked him for some advice, (not for money, there would be no point as he's a Yorkshireman), but he never even returned my call or my letter. Don't be fooled by titles.

My sister Rachael and her daughter come back from London with a nice story. They met with the singer, Russell Watson, who was diagnosed with a brain tumour and survived against the odds. They swapped stories, both intertwined with an ironclad belief and trust in God. When the conversation came to an end, Russell left Rachael with this, "David will recover."

Chapter 48

It's the small details in life that very often have the biggest impact. For instance, I have never had to pay cash for petrol before. My business card or company account at local stations enabled me to operate cashless. I can't even recover the cost of petrol against my expenses. A minor change you might think, but it's a daily reminder that our finances are evaporating, fast.

To raise funds, Dad is desperately calling East Anglian businesses who might need storage and Hugh is hoping to raise monies by selling farm buildings ripe for development. Personally I have no idea how we can cope as things are. Yet still I am unfazed, I ask for advice when I pray and I'm told not to worry. So I don't.

Chapter 49

Friday, a cold November morning, from my bedroom window I can see the last few clumps of purple and mustard foliage hanging on defiantly to the huge beech tree to the right of our lawn.

Still in a daze from the chemo and the radio, each and every day feels like a triumph, occasionally interlaced with scary reminders of reality. Chest pain, weird black-and-white flickering in my eyes, breathing difficulties, numbness down one side of my body, mega toothache. Sometimes all of these things come at the same time, and I sort of collapse where I'm standing, (I call it reconnecting), it takes me down and crushes my confidence for a minute or two.

Prayer picks me up and dusts me down, the little voice in my head reassures me that all of this is part of recovery.

Sunday, I flick through a couple of pages of the Sunday times. In my past life, I would read the business section cover to cover, all I can manage today is my horoscope. I never read horoscopes, but here goes:

'Be thankful for your intuition which is telling you that the disarray around you and, to a certain extent, in your own life is all about progress. However, maintaining that optimism means having the discipline to ignore those around you who behave like 'chicken little' and declare the sky is falling. The positive changes that are coming require swift and dramatic shifts in both the lives of individuals and of institutions. Some of what's worthwhile is already appearing. Focus on those developments and, when you're asked to join others in a bean-feast, particularly around Friday's emotionally intense full moon, decline politely and dwell instead on harbingers of a fabulous future'

I couldn't make this stuff up if I wanted to.

December, and I find myself in the dentist's chair having root canal treatment. I haven't been seen in public for a while, I feel very self-conscious because I look so shit, but I make it to the surgery with a narrow smile glued onto my face.

The treatment is hard for me to endure, the injections, the fierce drilling, the constant threat of a reconnection taking me out, the whole experience is unpleasant to say the least.

On the way home, I do have another 'reconnection', this time it feels as if 1,000,000 Volts are passing through my body as I wriggle about in the front seat. Later in the afternoon, Danielle calls an emergency doctor because my temperature spikes at 39°, much to my delight, he diagnoses an ear infection.

Over the next few days, I cower beneath the bed sheets, waiting for the next reconnection to hit. Danielle is constantly calling my specialist as more temperature spikes, dizziness, dry eye, mega indigestion, head pain and now back pain, attack my body and mind. This is definitely a two steps forward and the three back type of situation. My specialist Sarah remains nonplussed, thank God.

It would have been helpful if the doctors had warned me about these after effects, but the fact is that every patient is different, physiologically, psychologically and also physically. Also every tumour is unique, so in medical terms this all adds up to a pile of unknowns.

Chapter 50

Cambridge. Fresh from another brain scan, Sarah is umming and ahhing about whether or not to give me another course of chemo,

"It's that little shadow there," she points out on her laptop screen, "remember, we talked about it before?"

Mum and Dad, Hugh and Danielle we all wear blank expressions, nobody remembers a shadow being mentioned, it's the sort of thing you remember, but hey ho, I have to be cured.

"Bring it on." I tell her, and we walk out of the hospital armed with more little capsules.

Back at base camp Pastor O calls for an update. He too is unphased but he tells me how authorities refused to extend his visa so he must go home to Nigeria. Bummer. There's not a lot I can do, but I contact various government departments offering to sponsor him, but hear nothing back from any of them. I am well aware that Nigerians have, let's say, a mixed reputation, but to tarnish every single individual with the same brush, inevitably leads to gentle souls like Pastor O being discriminated against. The hospital shooed him off and now immigration has done the same. Pity.

Chapter 51

I have always loved Christmas. I'm too exhausted to make the school Christmas carol concert this year, so I stay back, lay still on the settee, wearing only a dressing gown, in the shadows of a crackling fire and read Armstrong's captivating and brilliant book 'every second counts' as the outside temperature dives to minus 4°.

When I was a child, Christmas was all about more and more expensive presents, in my teens and 20s it was about partying as well. Since then, Christmas became the season our customers expected to be rewarded for the business they had put our way over the last 12 months. The more lavish and generous we were, the more business seemed to come over the following 12 months and so on. One buyer wants a car, a range Rover maybe, another needs the cash. I don't say they didn't do their job well, they were always hard and mean and ruthless, but a Christmas box earned you first shout at the business on offer. We couldn't risk reining in the perks, and our customers got more and more greedy as trade increased.

All of a sudden it's Christmas week, the atmosphere is full of excitement and expectation. The girls have their friends popping in and out of the house. Uncles, aunts, in laws and a handful of close friends bring nicely wrapped gifts of all shapes and sizes. Christmas songs are piped around the house and all four dogs take enormous liberties sensing it's holiday time.

I call my surgeon friend Mamoun and ask him for advice. A new pain in my left leg is rapidly moving up into first place on the pain and suffering league table. Initially, I write it off as just another side effect from the treatment but the pain in my left groin and has an eerie intensity about it. Mamoun insists on coming round to see me, he is confused by the growing pain and puts me on the fast-track for an ultrasound which will be done the following day.

Tonight in bed I moan to Danielle with an unusual regularity, finally causing her to put down the book she is reading, aptly titled 'The secret diary of a demented housewife'. She dishes out more painkillers and gets back into her book.

By morning, I am exhausted from an agonising sleepless night. I hate, hate, hate to cause another commotion, but I know for certain I need to get to a hospital.

I stubbornly refuse to call an ambulance, so Danielle brings the car round to the front door. I sit up in bed, still dressed in the tracksuit I didn't have the energy to take off the night before and hobble out of the bedroom. The first step on the long and graceful staircase is a whole new division of agony, not just a man's agony, this is real agony, 10 on the agony scale, so rudy painful I am creased up on the hall floor unable to move a muscle. I collapse, I can't do another inch.

The ambulance slowly draws up to our large front door, I can make out the sound of gravel pinging and popping beneath its tyres. The calm crew, one male and one female, bring calm and positivity to where I am lying huddled on the floor. Danielle talks through the symptoms and I am given gas and air which I draw in deep breaths. What a relief, what a buzz and finally, euphoria. I start dreaming about a friend, he's a Jew, he's a lawyer, he's the same age as me and right now he is skiing in Canada where he has his own chalet.

Only weeks ago I was green with envy, he has better cars, more expensive properties, and a boat moored in Puerto Banus. He has more.

Now, in my dream, I'm looking at him from a different angle. He is on his third unhappy marriage, with one young daughter who he only gets to see from time to time. I couldn't bear that.

Back to reality and I'm looking up to see Emily and Hannah and Danielle, smiling bravely and wiping their tears away. I wouldn't swap places with him for all the tea in China.

By the end of the day, I am full of painkillers, I'm not thinking in any coherent way and I slide in and out of sleep between bouts of intense pain.

By the time early evening comes, I find myself in a ward pleading and then arguing with a nurse who is refusing to increase my painkillers or give me a solution to the intolerable pain. I am so desperate, I scream at the top of my voice for help, over and over again.

When help finally arrives in the form of a duty doctor, I am given what he refers to as 'an elephant's portion' finally passing out completely.

Once again, doctors and nurses are puzzled.

Later, I'm not sure what time of the day or night it is but a rushed ultrasound confirms a massive DVT in my left leg. All I know is that these things can be fatal if they head north. The duty doctor doesn't mince his words.

"It's a miracle (his words not mine) this one hasn't moved," he points out.

Too much information. But the reference to a miracle sits well with me...

Is it morning? Apparently a superbug outbreak in the main hospital threatens to confine me to this ward. A kind friend Dr Mathialagen moves quickly in order to transfer me to the adjoining private hospital where I'm given a comfortable room to myself and quarantined. A pain management program is hurriedly set up and the drugs begin melting the clot.

I've been saved again.

The flipside is that this month's chemo cycle has to be delayed, but to defuse the time bomb in my leg it's a small price to pay.

Chapter 52

Still hospitalised, Christmas and New Year are both a bit of a blur for me. Danielle tries hard to keep everything as normal as possible, for Emily and Hannah's sake in particular. At the forefront of my mind is the knowledge I am fighting for my life on two fronts now. But I'm so thankful to be alive at all, having not one, but two life threatening conditions leaves me wondering what the heck is coming next.

I don't have to wait long to find out.

9th January

Danielle visits in the morning. There is exciting news, Sarah, on her return from a skiing trip, announces that I am cleared for chemo again.

This very good news is diluted with the results from the latest scan. There is a new discovery, a schwannoma in my pelvic area. Where it's come from and when, is another mystery. Sarah is pretty sure it's 'benign' but it has to be investigated.

Shit.

This is a good time to pray.

Chapter 53
Home Sweet Home

There's a saying that things happen in threes. Today turns out to verify this old wives' tale.

Dad borrows the Range Rover because he wants to take a ride around his farm before getting stuck into some work over there. He's always in a bit of a rush to get into work, and the wheels spin in the gravel as the car lurches forward. I am in the kitchen with Mum and Hugh, and we give one another a wry smile as we hear the roar of the powerful engine disappear into the distance.

So when Hugh spots Dad marching back up the driveway towards the house, we can but wonder what he's up to. Dad only ever walks on a golf course, and judging by his ruby red, fixed expression, we are expecting the worst. He bustles into the kitchen cursing the car for breaking down. Mum, Hugh and I try to keep straight-faced. Fortunately Danielle's Lexus is here, a similar sort of car, which he is grateful to have the use of before the breakdown truck arrives.

After calming down, there's more spinning of the wheels, and he's gone again. We all laugh out loud, Dad is so impatient sometimes.

Meanwhile Mum insists on cooking a huge breakfast which nobody really wants. She's in maternal mode and I know she wants to do everything she can to help me recover, all the same, having cooked food shoved into your face all the time is testing.

Half an hour or so passes by before the heavy kitchen door swings open again, we can hardly believe our eyes. It's Dad, this time his face is purple with rage,

"Can you believe it!? The Lexus has packed up!" he rants, looking at each one of us, checking for any sniggering as we all bite our lip. His shoes are caked in mud, he's pretty exhausted and very cross.

Michelle, our long suffering nanny, bravely offers her services to drop Dad off in her car. Ironic isn't it, two modern, sophisticated, and it has to be said, expensive cars let you down, and it's a little old car worth nine pence that does the job. It is indeed, a very funny sight to see the two of them disappear down the driveway.

Only a few minutes pass by before the telephone rings, it's Michelle,

"You're never going to believe this..."

Chapter 54

In my time, I have written several unfinished bestsellers, and I've entered one or two national writing competitions. Don't they say we all have at least one book in us?

Each and every time I submit a sample of my work, I have no doubt whatsoever that the agent or publisher will rush to sign me up. I am always genuinely surprised when they don't. Ever.

I've just picked up an autobiography by Goldie Hawn 'The Lotus grows in the hand'. From page one I am hooked, the movement of the story, the flow of prose, the simple construction, I glide effortlessly through her life story, page after page after glorious page.

This wonderful story, written so beautifully, is dashing any hope I have of becoming a writer.

I'm a slow reader, and with all the medication I'm on right now, it's difficult for me to concentrate for long periods without falling asleep, but each time I surface, night or day, I reach for the dog-eared paperback. I love it, I realise I can't write as well as this.

I feel inadequate, just as I do when I see Bill Gates and his wife on the TV, giving away $30 billion for good causes. Wow. How do you compete with that?

But as I read all about Goldie Hawn, sleep a little and contemplate on all of this, I think about the messages

Hugh has taught me from the Bible, that each and every one of us has a separate journey. It's not about the money, or the fame or glory, and my reasons for becoming a writer were probably not in harmony with the plan God has for me.

This makes sense. It's rational, and it makes life easier because now I can see that if I was meant to be a writer and if my reasons for becoming a 'rich and famous' author were in accord with God's plan, then I'd be a rich and famous writer. Simple.

The purpose of writing this book is in the hope that it will give someone, somewhere, hope, strength and a belief that anything is possible. If it's published, all well and good, if it's not, no worries. I have more stories and ideas for more books, 'The Magic Pond in Muckleton', starring a bug, twin bluebottles, a hover fly and a jackdaw!

Understanding and accepting my life may or may not be programmed for literary success, fails to damp down my ambition to write. Writing gives me pleasure and satisfaction.

This evening Danielle receives a call from the Schwannoma specialist. It's another magical moment, thank God, the thing's not invading my spine. I had no idea that it might have done. No need for any additional treatment, just the chemo tabs and the daily stomach injection. Lovely.

Chapter 55

Sunday morning is cold and windy. I wake up shivering and stumble around the four poster bed to reset the temperature gauge on the far wall. I can hear the rattle of a woodpecker hammering ferociously in the woodland close to the house, I feel exhausted just listening to him.

I don't want to disturb Danielle, it's still early, so I begin the daily routine of pill popping, more accurately downing fourteen chemo capsules. I only do this five days out of every month, for six months. Sounds a drag but believe me, I thank God for it.

I slink back into the warmth of our giant bed. Ideas come flooding into my mind; commissioning Viscount Linley to design a range of garden furniture, a garden centre and a florist shop in Dubai and so on.

Some ideas are better than others, that's for sure, and there's the small matter of funding, especially at a time when the government has virtually bankrupt this country and when the banks are sinking beneath the billions of pounds they have incompetently and recklessly borrowed and loaned all over the world.

Nevertheless, as Winston Churchill famously said, 'we shall overcome'.

Today is 28th January, as is the norm at the moment, I slope around the house in a sort of trance. I exist, in an out-of-body sort of way, detached from everything. It is difficult to put into words.

Impatience is beginning to nibble away at my desire to get my life up and running again.

I have almost finished Goldie Hawn's book, in it she mentions how the Tibetans are the happiest people on Earth. But how is happiness measured, and what is it compared to? Anyway, the more I read, the more relevance it has to my own life.

By Friday, I am feeling quite unwell. More anti-nausea medicine and a reminder from Danielle of how she felt during pregnancy fails to do the trick. The next few days become a bit of a blur. I feel sick, I've got the shits, quite badly as it happens, and I can't bring myself to look at food. Just the smell of cooking in the house makes me want to throw up.

Dad spends more and more of his time clearing the warehouses in anticipation of a new tenant coming along. Mum spends much of her time fussing around me, and Danielle works hard to keep family life and her business life as normal as possible. Life has become a team effort rather than me leading the old, somewhat selfish existence, my whole 'raison d'etre' now is to pick myself up and enjoy life with Danielle and the girls.

Chapter 56

Early on Thursday morning, from my bedside I look out over the front garden and the meadow beyond. Nature lies cocooned beneath a bright, white blanket of snow. The sheep are standing still, appearing frozen to the spot, each with a coat of creamy coloured snow balancing on their flat, table top backs.

Danielle has gone downstairs to let the barking dogs out and I watch as Charlie and Fudge slip and slide across the lawn in hopeless pursuit of squirrels.

Twenty-four hours later and I'm beginning to feel much better, living on Weetabix, cheese and tomato sandwiches, and cans of mandarins. Business ideas continue to flood in; setting up a new local radio station; buying residential properties at auction, renovating and quickly reselling; developing sites for travellers throughout East Anglia. There's a constant flow of ideas spewing out of my mind, at the same time our seven figure mortgage begins to haunt me again, and a local contractor screws me for twenty grand.

Chapter 57

9th March, and a mate of mine (M) calls me to give some sobering news. A mutual friend, let's call him P, has been diagnosed with cancer of the liver, colon and lungs. He is 49 years old.

How would I describe P?

He's a winner. He travelled round the world as a backpacker when he was in his early 20s, and he's travelled around the world first-class ever since. He's made millions and lost them. And he's made them again. He is truly a one off, an extrovert, flamboyant on the outside, coy on the inside, people either love him or hate him, but if you love him, he's one of the most loyal friends a man can have. He travels back and forth from Norfolk to South Africa, he leads a jet set life together with his South African wife, and he loves his three girls.

"Do you think you could help," M asks, "he's shattered."

I am genuinely puzzled, P has a thousand 'friends' who would jump at the chance to get into P's good books. As if reading my mind, M continues,

"You know how inspirational you have been to him in the way you have handled your own problems, 'J' (P's wife), thinks you could help him cope with this."

I don't know how much help I can be, after all, I'm still taking a course of chemo and I look shit.

But I believe. I believe I'm going to get over this and live a normal life (whatever normal is). And I believe in our creator, God, I believe in Jesus, angels, heaven and miracles. Every day I pray, and I receive that reassurance. I know it's not my time.

"I'm terrified," P mumbles down the phone to me.

I am genuinely taken aback to hear this lion squeaking like a mouse,

"All I can do mate", I begin, "is tell you how it's been for me."

"David, that's all I ask, I know you'll give it me straight."

"P, you know the only thing that separates the two of us, is that I believe there is life after death, and you don't."

"A faith you mean?"

"Yea," I have to think about it, "a faith."

"Have you read the Old Testament?" he snaps.

"Err…," I'm already out of my depth, the little I do know about the Old Testament is that it's pretty brutal and dark. Maybe the world was a much darker place then and needed stricter control, I don't know. I do know there were loads of prophecies foretelling the coming of Jesus hundreds of years before it happened. For me, that alone is very powerful and convincing evidence to authenticate the Bible, maybe not word for word, I don't know, but it's a sound book that makes logical sense and gives good advice on how to live on this planet.

"Well I have", P's tone of voice has changed, "that has nothing to do with my idea of God. My God is a kind, caring God," he moans.

P's voice is bitter, full of disappointment, and understandably, fear. I tread very carefully over the next twenty-five minutes, during which time I manage to get him into a much stronger and positive frame of mind and P signs off with,

"That is the best talk I've ever had."

Chapter 58

24th March, we travel to Cambridge to get the results of a recent MRI scan and to collect my fourth batch of Temo. The temptation is to feel terrified, to ask myself, what if this, what if that? But what would be the point? I have no control over what the scans will show, all that keeps me together is the reassurance I get through prayer. That's my only shield, and I'm calm because of that, but it doesn't stop me having butterflies in my stomach as Sarah closes the door behind her, sits down at her computer and begins to talk,

"I am very good at reading scans," she boasts, we're all on the edges of our seats, "and there are colleagues of mine who might read these scans negatively," she warns, turning the screen of her laptop slightly towards us, "this is what we're looking at, here and here," she goes on. Not one of us is concentrating on the screen, we are all tense, sitting upright and bracing ourselves for what she might say next,

"These scans look good, I assure you."

Dad, Mum, Danielle, everyone to drop their heads with deep relief before the tears come. I feel my tears waiting, excitement holds them back. Thank you God, thank you Jesus, thank you, thank you, thank you.

On our way out we collect more chemo tabs, apparently there is a problem over supply, so I'm issued twenty smaller capsules for each day, instead of the usual four. Do I care? Do I heck. I would take a hundred or a thousand if I had to.

On the journey home, morale is high and it's great to see Dad and Mum more relaxed. Dad is always positive, always light-hearted, but I've noticed subtle changes in him, the glint in his eye is missing its sparkle; and Mum, she is constantly fretting and looks, well, strained. All of this has taken its toll, both of them have told me separately, "I wish I could swap places with you," they both mean it because they feel helpless and want so much for me to be well again. Often, when I am praying, I ask that they will both live for another ten years, by that time Dad will be ninety-two or so and my mum will be eighty-five I think. I can't imagine life without either of them. They are *so* full of life and young at heart, I am complete with them, and I can't imagine life without either of them.

I go to bed with my mind spinning, today has been such a relief, I didn't know what to expect and I can't help but wonder about the poor buggers sitting opposite their specialists and getting bad news, when actually it might be good news if only their scans had been interpreted correctly. I'm lucky to have Sarah.

My last thoughts of the day regurgitate my financial worries, but as always, the calming voice in my head when I am praying, tells me to chill out, relax. So I do.

Chapter 59

In our desperation to find a solution to our financial problems, Danielle and I continue to rack our brains for a practical solution. Actually any solution would do. Yesterday, we asked our financial advisor to look into my pension policies, it's a bit of a long shot, but we need some sort of a miracle here.

Today is Good Friday and I feel well enough to take Danielle and the girls to Burnham Market horse trials. Just to be a family together is so enjoyable. I savour every moment.

As the horses thunder past, Danielle's telephone rings, actually it quacks like a duck, and she turns away to find a quiet spot to talk. The girls and I walk a short way up the hill to take a closer position near to the water jump.

When Danielle catches up with us, breathless and excited, I can tell she's got good news.

"Darling, you've turned fifty, you can take out 25% of one of your policies, tax free!" Danielle is acting like we've just won the lottery, holding hands and dancing with the girls, meanwhile my jaw drops I'm left speechless for a moment. I gesture with my hand for her to hurry up and give me the number, "Sorry, I'm so excited, I can't even remember how much it is, £300,000 I think, or £500,000 maybe?"

Neither of us care how much it is, all that's important is now we have some breathing space, time for me to get better and to create an income somehow.

For a minute or two, we all do a pretty good impression of Morris dancing before I put my hands together and look up to the sky, "Thank you."

Chapter 60

I'm watching an episode of the secret millionaire on TV. This is a programme about giving, and I am fascinated with it. Today's episode features 'Donna's dream house', a charity for children who are suffering from life threatening illnesses. 'Len' and his wife lost their daughter a couple of years back and decided to handle their grief by helping other children in similar situations. They use their Blackpool home to accommodate children and their families so that they can have a few quality days in a holiday atmosphere. For some families, this is their first family holiday ever, for many others it's the last, but it gives these children and their families some good memories to cherish.

I am so moved by this programme, even before the credits roll I've made up my mind to register our own charity. Daniella's family has a holiday house in Hunstanton on the Norfolk coast which we can use and we will call the charity The Hunny Trust. Job done.

Chapter 61

Today is Dad's birthday, 1st May, and he's decided to hold a party. He loves parties. To see him, you would never guess he's eighty odd years old. Today he spends much of his time entertaining his grandchildren by removing his false teeth and scrunching up his face like a ball of waste paper. All the children are running around him screaming, partly with delight and partly in fear of the monstrous faces he pulls. When he's not doing that, he is showing adults a shocking photograph of an emaciated dog (from an RSPCA flyer) claiming the dog is his. The more appalling the reaction, mainly from women, the funnier he finds it.

Inside the marquee, the air is warm and the afternoon sun lights up the party as if it were a summers day. It's perfect for the hundred or so family and friends to scoff the fine champagne and locally caught fish.

Dad's venue of choice is the Hoste Arms, P's one hundred bed boutique-style hotel in Burnham market. P is here of course, but he looks kind of shell-shocked, quiet, not like him at all. Normally he's working the room, gliding from person to person, but today his expression is one of emptiness and it's not long before he leaves to go home.

We take an early bath ourselves as we have a children's party to get the girls to.

When we pitch up, late of course, I'm a bit taken aback by how much weight Daniel has lost. Daniel and Louise are hosting the party, we are good friends with them and Daniel can take a good joke. I greet him with typical irreverence.

"How's it hanging you skinny bugger?" I ask.

"I'm feeling okay, but I can't have any more chemo now," he tells me. "I probably haven't got long, David." Understandably his tone is sombre and tinted with regret but I refuse to be reeled into his uncharacteristic negativity. All the same, this is sobering news. Six years ago, I didn't know him then, he was diagnosed with a tumour on his heart. At the time he was what you'd call a 'highflyer' in the city, living in the fast lane and making plenty of money. He was stopped in his tracks, when doctors told him he had up to four months left.

Today, his jacket looks two sizes too big for him, and his face is lined with defeat.

"There must be new drugs coming through," I tell him, trying to rally his spirits.

"Yes, there are medical advancements," he says, perking up a little, "but I'm on dialysis three times a week now, and it's all taking its toll David."

I leave the party, thankful I'm not in his shoes.

Chapter 62

I have my first workout with Hugh, a few press ups, a few sit ups, nothing too energetic, but it's a start, physically and mentally. My chemo is behind me and Sarah is pleased with my results.

On the 27th May, we get a call from our financial advisor. Hallelujah! Another policy stumps up believing I'm about to croak. This time another six figure sum arrives to shore up our dire finances, "Ask and you shall receive," I half joke to Danielle.

I scrunch both fists deep into my eye sockets, then pinch myself to check if this is real. Hugh is with us, looking as excited as we are and he knowingly recites a line from the Bible, Luke 1 vs 37, "Nothing is impossible with God."

I have to admit, all of this feels like there is something or someone looking over me, I'm not sure I deserve all these miracles, but I know that without them I wouldn't be here now.

May nudges June, normal life is inching its way back into my body. We all travel to London to see Hannah and her classmates singing in the Royal Albert Hall, and this evening I go for my first jog with Hugh, just for ten minutes or so. I still have the odd 'flutter' or 'reconnection', which strike me in the back like a knife and put me down for thirty seconds or so. They are less and less frequent and I see them as part of my recovery.

July begins with a trip to Cambridge to hear the results of my recent scan. I throw any apprehension or worry to the back of my mind, to consider anything but positive news would be to suggest I do not believe that someone up there is taking care of me. I walk into Sarah's office wearing my normal happy expression.

When we all come out, a handful of her words are ringing in my ears, 'perfect and delighted' are just two of the superlatives she uses, and all of the family are euphoric as we trek back home.

Robert, our friendly vicar, visits each week to give Hugh and me a Bible class. I have a lot of questions which Robert finds easy to deal with. Hugh, on the other hand, digs deeper, 'that's a great question' Robert keeps repeating, and each session we have together I find really interesting. The prophecies fascinate me, to have predicted so much, so accurately, hundreds of years before Jesus arrived, blows my mind.

Saturday, and I come across a TV program all about the life of Warren Buffet, one of the wealthiest men on this Earth. He is busy re-distributing his wealth to good causes and lives by the adage, 'I came into the world with nothing and I shall leave with nothing'. His children are well grounded and sensible individuals with no designs on their father's wealth whatsoever. He's told them to expect nothing. Through God's eyes this family must represent what he envisaged at the beginning, what a perfect concept. How I wish that I can do this with my life. I have the will, I just need the money part ...

New business ideas are popping up night and day. Recently I saw a man lying in a hospital bed wearing mini vibrator pads to prevent blood clots (why oh why was I not given these?). But these particular pads look heavy and not very portable. There must be a market for patients and air travellers around the world, for a portable version, so I put this on the mounting pile of new business ideas, 'development of a lightweight, battery or solar powered vibration set', at a good price of course'.

Chapter 63

Monday. Dad is back home after a brief spell in hospital. We sit around his bed listening to his shallow breathing, watching as his chest slowly half rises before quickly falling down to rest. Each intake of breath comes almost as a surprise, with longer and longer intervals between each one. We are all preparing ourselves for the inevitable.

All we can do today is take turns comforting and kissing him, taking hold of his big, soft hands with their thick fingers and manicured nails.

Some of my earliest memories are of those hands, gripping my own, stopping me from falling as I stumble, never failing to be there for me.

What will I do now? What will Mum do?

Rachael lights another crackling fire in the faint hope that we might get Dad back in the room again, but as the wind whistles around the house and the rain rattles against the glass windows, that prospect becomes more and more remote,

"What time is it?" Dad suddenly erupts.

"Six thirty," we all chime in.

"Quick, I need a wee."

We have a well-rehearsed routine for Dad's calls of nature, where the females scuttle out of the room while Hugh or myself put a plastic bottle into position.

"Let the trumpet sound!" Dad croaks, helping us through the moment.

"You know lads, there's a funny side to just about everything, even this."

Chapter 64

A few months earlier with money in the bank and recovery in the air, there was nothing else for it, other than to splash out on a fantastic adventure for all the family.

After much debate, we decided to travel by sleeper train through France and all the way down to the South of Spain, where Mum and Dad are holidaying in their apartment.

To make this adventure really special, we make it a three-centre trip, first we will have a night with Mum and Dad in the apartment, then we'll move on to a five star hotel called La Quinta nearby, and then we move a few kilometres further along the Costa Del Sol to a Ritz Carlton hotel reputed to be the world's best, Villa Padierna.

That's quite a boast, but I can tell you it's pretty special, a couple of years ago we went there to have a look. In fact we took afternoon tea there, you have to see this amazing building to believe it, with its Roman columns, fountains and waterfalls, it is something else. This is what the brochure claims, 'built in the traditional style of Italian villas of Tuscany, Villa Padierna towers over a beautiful golf course called Los Flamingos, 18 manicured fairways painting the landscape in vivid green. Boasting a three star Michelin chef, heated pools, tennis courts and a thermal spa.' Sounds too good to be true, doesn't it? When something sounds too good to be true, it usually is.

So 17th July, a people carrier arrives early morning to take us to the local train station. The driver is old and grey, so it falls to us to load up, while he sits back and reads the Daily Mail. Danielle has agreed to limit baggage due to the various train changes we have en route, but as more and more cases come out, I'm feeling a bit miffed, especially as we have to crush my small 'crew' case in order to close down the rear door.

To add to the problem, Hugh turned up with a huge black body bag, "We're going for nearly a month you know," he protests when he senses my irritation.

When we set off in the overloaded vehicle, the girls start to sing Cliff Richards', 'Summer Holiday', and any frustration I might have had evaporates.

Once at King's Cross we heave the bags across the road to St Pancras station. Nobody is in the mood yet to crack jokes about this monumental struggle we are having with fourteen various bags and cases, but once we sit down in the Eurostar train heading for the Gare Du Nord station in Paris, we are all excited about the journey ahead.

Two hours and ten minutes of high speed travel, and we come to an abrupt halt in the countryside. For a few moments everything goes very quiet, then one or two voices begin to break the silence, and soon all the passengers have turned to one another and are speculating what the problem might be. Almost thirty minutes pass by before an announcement crackles through the public address system,

"This is your conductor speaking, we are very sorry for this short delay which is due to a fire close to the tracks."

It's not long before mutterings of discontent begin to reverberate through the carriage, 'not the leaves then' and 'that's a new one' and 'short delay, we'll believe that when we see it', there's a general unrest and an air of mistrust.

We hastily start to recalculate our plans, there's not a great deal of tolerance with all of the connecting trains we need to catch, even half an hour makes us all a bit jittery.

Almost an hour passes by, our coach is becoming unbearably hot and passengers around us are talking of smashing windows as the temperature rises. A middle-aged business woman wearing a yellow summer dress and holding open her laptop, runs up and down the carriage exposing her massive calves, inviting everybody to comment on this disaster. She is apparently broadcasting this in a blog. None of us think to ask her what the point of this might be.

Finally a conductor marches through the train opening doors and windows to allow some cooler air into the carriages, and a few minutes later, news comes over the loud speaker of our imminent departure.

By the time we reach Paris, our plans are in tatters. We are forced to find a hotel for the night which is incredibly inconvenient and also expensive. Initially, Eurostar promises the minimum of recompense, then retracts it. A letter will be winging itself to Eurostar when we get back.

Despite this, morale is high, after all, this is an adventure and it feels liberating for me, away from doctors, hospitals and anything associated with my old way of life.

Eurostar organise a hotel for the night, it's just around the corner from the station but too far to walk with all of our luggage, so we find a taxi and begin to load up. When the driver realises how short this journey will be, he curls his lip in disappointment. He steadfastly refuses to allow five passengers into his spacious vehicle, so we are forced to hail an extra taxi for the three or four minute journey. Frogs, can't live with 'em, can't live without 'em.

Once outside the hotel, we struggle to unload the baggage while the two drivers huddle together in deep conversation, one is tilting his flat cap backwards and forwards and the other is shrugging his shoulders and opening his arms in a wide arc. We pretty much know what's coming, but we are too tired to put up a fight when the crazy bill comes in.

Danielle talks with the hotel concierge to reorganise the next leg of our journey. No trains before tomorrow evening, so in true British spirit we all decide to make the best of it and plan a day visiting museums and sightseeing.

After a piss poor continental breakfast, we set out on foot to Notre Dame, and then the Musee D'Orsay where we have lunch. We seem to walk miles, the blistering heat gradually wearing all of us down, and by late afternoon we have had enough. None of us can face the walk back so we begin to look for a taxi. Hugh uses the Metro for the short trip to La Gare D'Austerlitz.

A small army of blind taxi drivers hurtle past as we stand together beneath a scorching sun. By the time we meet up with Hugh at the station, over €60 has been wrenched from our pockets, and all of us are exhausted, again.

"What kept you?" Hugh moans when we finally catch up with him over an hour later.

Only when he hears how much the taxi fare was, does he smile, the Metro ticket looks good value at €1.50.

If we miss this train, we will have to wait another 24 hours for the next one, so we hurriedly buy a few prepacked sandwiches, which cost a small fortune, and make our way along the busy platform and onto the train.

We are all looking forward to sleeping in the luxury of first-class accommodation, hopefully we'll get a few hours of solid sleep on our way to Madrid.

A booking error leaves Hugh in a cramped carriage with three backpackers, none of whom speak any English. Our cabin is not much better, tiny, cramped and hardly what you would call the 'first-class accommodation' we paid for.

Originally we booked adjoining rooms with Hugh, so we insist he sleeps in our cabin. In the excitement of cramming all of us in together like this, we all have lots of laughs. The beds are no more than narrow plastic shelves, two on each side of the cabin, one above the other. Danielle and Hannah somehow manage to balance on one, while Emily, Hugh and I have the dubious luxury of a bed each.

The high-speed train rockets through station after station, it's too uncomfortable to fall into any meaningful sleep, only the monotonous clickety-clack of steel on steel calms the mind and brings on a restful semi-sleep.

In the middle of the night, one of Hugh's magnificent farts blasts out like a trumpet, it wakes all of us, 'sorry' he shouts above the noise, before we all laugh ourselves back into our shallow semi-sleep.

Fourteen uncomfortable hours later we reach Madrid, tired but happy, and transfer to another superfast train. By now, the novelty of travelling by train has begun to wane. Finally we pull into Malaga station where we encounter another slight hitch to our plans in that we can't hire a car because there aren't any to hire. The banks are in the shit, so there's no money to lend the car hire companies to purchase new vehicles. Hola! Spain.

But we find a taxi anyway and soon enough we are merrily spinning along the carretera towards Marbella where Mum and Dad are waiting for us.

Chapter 65

It's Friday, a little after nine. Dad has chilled champagne on standby and Mum has prepared her signature dish, a beef stew, for our arrival. Home cooking, there's nothing like it, and by the time we sink into our comfortable beds we are well fed, watered and totally knackered.

My father believes he is uniquely blessed with a rare talent to mimic the crow of the cock. Six hours after hitting the pillow we are rudely awakened to the cock crowing accompanied by his tuneless, almost string-less guitar as he walks the marble covered corridors. Buenos Dias Dad....

We spend a leisurely morning together with Mum and Dad before being ferried to La Quinta hotel, only five minutes away. Danielle and the girls are clearly excited to see the entire Aston Villa football team are here, there's a beautiful swimming pool and various restaurants to try.

The first night we make a small error, paying a premium to sit at the top table in the Japanese restaurant. 'Chef' furiously chops meat and vegetables with his ceremonial knives and then griddles eggs which he adds to the mix before spraying us all with fine pieces of his concoction. Hannah, with her allergy to eggs, is horrified, but we manage to finish the meal despite her threats of a walkout.

But we have a fun week here. Some days we spend our time with Mum and Dad at the apartment, sometimes they come to the hotel, in fact one night they both stay with us overnight while their air conditioning is being fixed.

I have a minor flutter due to overheating, but it's soon over and forgotten. The hotel is very good, but we fully expect La Padierna to surpass this hotel on every level.

As the days go by, the holiday vibe mellows and relaxes all of us, before we know it we are firmly installed in La Padierna.

I've got to admit, this final leg of our adventure turns out to be a bit of an anti-climax, even dare I say, a major disappointment. The irony is that we would have been more than happy in a basic hotel or dossing down with Mum and Dad. We are happy as a family, it's not about a building, it's about being together, and when, finally, we get back to home sweet home, an e-mail is waiting for me from La Padierna inviting customer feedback, oh there's a special offer as well.

By now, my business head is gathering steam again, and I have the time on my hands to respond. Often, the measure of a business comes down to whether you listen to customers, I'm interested to see their response to my letter, which reads like this:

Dear Patricia, (Head of Customer Services)

Thank you for your invitation to comment on our recent holiday experience in the hotel La Padierna. I hope you will find the following information helpful and constructive.

1.   First and foremost I would like to compliment you and your colleagues from the manager down, for HIS professionalism and attention to detail in most areas of the business. However, the high standard of care he aimed to provide, fell some way short in the catering department as a direct result of your policy to hire inexperienced trainees for seasonal work.

For instance, the breakfast experience fell way short of what we received at the Westin Hotel only a few kilometres away. And the pool bar, where we specifically ordered a club sandwich without egg due to our youngest daughter's allergy, yet were served egg sandwiches. We sent them back of course but to make matters worse, the waiter came back from the kitchen with egg sandwiches, dangerous! You will understand why we were not pleased when the waiter attempted to charge us for the sandwiches.

Could I also mention, the choice of meals for children is very limited, and the so-called fresh fruit drinks served around the pool are made up from frozen syrup, sugar and water. They taste revolting, and at seven euros are wildly overpriced. In the main restaurant, chicken meals were sent back to the kitchen but we still got billed.

2.   In the swimming pool, I had to rescue two individuals; a small boy had a bad slip on one of the marble areas around the pool in all we counted four similar incidents with adults slipping on the marble surround to the pool, one of those being a lifeguard on duty. The swimming pool looks lovely but it's freakin' dangerous. Again I had to help an elderly lady who got herself into trouble because she couldn't grip onto the pool edges; if you were to fit a small handrail it could save

a life, we saw several elderly people and also small children struggling in the same way.

3. Our air conditioning was never fixed despite three calls to maintenance on the first and second days. Also sharp screws were protruding on the plate beneath the room door, again these were never fixed. The service lift close to our room was noisy, and we couldn't get Sky TV. Your manager organised a DVD player to compensate, which we were grateful for.

4. We were keen to play tennis with our children at the facilities you infer are available. The tennis club turns out to be quite remote from the hotel with no transport available to get us there. One of your staff at the front desk suggested we walk, which as you know would be a long (one hour?) and dangerous journey, we would never dream of taking our children for a walk along this road.

5. We visited the spa complex and looked at your indoor pool. Thank God, we didn't jump in. The water was extremely hot. No attendant was on duty, and the temperature of the water would scald anybody who jumped in. In my opinion, it would be a very good idea to prevent children from entering the room and also to inform adults of the dangers.

I hope you will find all my comments constructive and I look forward to your response in the near future.

They never reply.

Chapter 66

Summer submits to autumn and on 1st September, unexpected news arrives. The second policy we hoped would pay out, refuses to pay a single peso. With the latest info from Sarah, they guess I'm going to last at least until 2025 in which case they won't have to pay out the six figure sum.

Far from being disappointed, we celebrate. I am banking on them being right.

Christmas and New Year celebrations are a warm mixture of family time beside log fires and walks over the snow-covered countryside. I treasure every moment.

Dad's skin turned bright yellow recently and now he's been diagnosed with cancer of the pancreas. Fuck. The words 'I wish I could swap places with you son' are ringing in my ears.

We all mobilise into another fighting force against the odds, quickly tracking down a top Harley Street specialist for a second opinion. We rush down to London.

"There are options, Mr Sadar tells us, 'Wipple' surgery after chemotherapy is very much the choice of leading experts right now, but there are risks...and the operation is equivalent to having a head on high speed car crash."

We reel back in our plush seats.

Dad is adamant he wants a good quality of life without the agony of risky major surgery, which may, or may not give him any extra time.

I can't bear the thought of losing Dad, I know the whole family feels the same way, it would be a shocking tragedy for all of us. I want to be sick.

3rd January one of Emily's school friends is desperate to show us her Chihuahua puppies. Bearing in mind we already have Charlie and Fudge, we all agree to resist any temptation to buy a puppy. It would be madness, we're not doggie people anyway, we were given Charlie and Fudge, and much as we love them, they're more than a handful. We will win the Euro lottery twice before we have another dog.

Sunday the 10th, Paris and Hope, our new Chihuahua puppies, are delivered by Fiona and Alex, the breeders. There's much excitement as we welcome the puppies into their new home. While the children make a fuss of the dogs, Danielle and I chat with Fiona and Alex who we met for the first time a few days ago. It quickly transpires that Fiona believes she has a gift, as a faith healer. She believes her gift is God-given and offers to perform a healing ritual for me, right here and now.

Never one to look a gift horse in the mouth, I readily agree, and she gets to work, using her hands to gently press on areas of my head, neck and shoulders. We move into the main hallway, away from all the squeals of joy and excitement.

I am sitting upright, on a high backed armchair, Fiona is on her knees facing me.

Peace and tranquillity. I close my eyes and listen as she mutters in whispered tones. I can't make out what

168

she's saying but there is a calmness around the two of us, I like it.

Fiona is away with the fairies.

Suddenly she begins to speak, the tone of her voice is different, lower, rough around the edges, her eyes are closed.

"David, you have a long journey ahead of you. You're not going anywhere – God expects great things from you."

We both open our eyes, Fiona begins talking.

"Does any of this mean anything to you?" she asks in a quiet voice.

I hesitate before giving the answer, I can only tell her the truth,

"Yes it does, I pray every day, I know for a fact that God created everything, I talk to Jesus constantly." She is looking directly into my eyes, I can see tears welling up, not of pain, but of pleasure. "Fiona, I have been given a second chance at life, I wasn't a particularly nice person before all of this happened. I had a few bob but I was never satisfied, never fulfilled, and I had everything that's important, a beautiful wife, two beautiful girls, a loving family, but I didn't appreciate it. I do now. When I pray, I ask for the only things that are important to me. I ask God to restore my health, I ask him to allow me the time to help Emily and Hannah grow up, to see them safely married, to get to know their children if they have any, I pray for time I suppose. And I pray for guidance, because I feel that I have a purpose in life, why else would Jesus save me time after time? I have a feeling, don't ask me to describe it, but a sense that I will do great things in this life."

Fiona takes hold of both my hands, she's smiling.

"Don't you worry David, I'll keep sending the Angels out to you", she promises, "and to your dad."

Chapter 67

Dad has his first chemo session today, 29th January. I'm numb, if I'm honest, I'm scared, he's such a big part of my life.

It's vital, for all our sakes, we remain positive and back him up all the way. Work is the best distraction and antidote where Dad is concerned. Over the following months, we focus on maximising every asset we have, the most valuable of which is a fifty acre site in the middle of our village. Surrounded by two schools, a housing estate and a new health centre, the site is ripe for development.

We engage the services of a specialist Q.C. and by the end of May we're ready to submit our substantial application. It's a 'que sera sera' moment for the family, I hope for Dad's sake it comes off, he's always referred to the site as 'the jewel in the crown', and he has a vision of residential, light industrial and retail units, everything the village needs.

The month of June kicks off with a spell of warm sunny weather. A week or two back, my right leg and two of my fingers began to feel numb. Sarah's not phased (as always), she guesses it might be debris floating about after the radiotherapy. No worries then.

The Hunny Trust is now a registered charity. It's no mean feat to be officially registered by the charity commission, and I've got Danielle to thank for that.

The only slight blot on the landscape is Leung Sing, locally known as Ernie. He is a true friend of mine, I have known him many years, I've trashed his Chinese restaurant more times than I care to remember and he's always laughed it off. He is the genuine article, I never understand a word he says, but I love the skinny little man.

Anyway, he's just told me there's a growth on his liver.

Chapter 68

August, time for my MRI scans and a chat with Sarah. When we meet, she is her positive and philosophical self.

"I'm not unduly worried," she starts, "you remember I showed you the other subtle mark near to the tumour?" she asks casually,

"Eer, no," (as if I would forget),

"The mark or shadow you can see there," she's turned the laptop screen towards me and is pointing to a small area with her slim Mont Blanc. I have all the usual suspects with me, who remain completely silent and lean forwards in their seats to get a better view of the black-and-white images of my brain.

"I would say it's necrosis... but it could be another tumour."

"What's necrosis when it's at home?" I ask gingerly.

"Sort of, debris from the radiotherapy," she tells me quite casually, "I'm thinking it may be sensible to have another short course of Temozolomide, what do you think?"

She is looking me straight in the eye, giving me the look I have learnt to trust.

I can feel my heart thumping like a hammer on steel, my mind is spinning, images of Emily and Hannah's happy faces flash up in front of my eyes, I want to burst into tears.

Instantaneously, someone, I guess it's Jesus, takes over, and yanks the controls to steady my mind. The message is simple. 'Do not worry, God has a good plan for me, not a bad one.'

"Good, when do I start?"

A few days pass before our friend P suddenly throws the towel in. During his last week, he had two really bizarre experiences. He 'crossed over' into what he described as 'a happy white world', he wasn't allowed to say any more, but those experiences transformed him, left him calm, almost happy to be moving on.

Chapter 69

I can't lie, to find myself back on the Temozolomide, well it's a tad disappointing and I don't understand it. No worries but I didn't expect it.

But I've learned that God's plan for me is unpredictable yet totally reliable. I trust him implicitly. So when my insurers learn I'm back on the Temo again, they change their minds, I am, according to their stats, about to die after all. Instantly, we have a serious wedge of money in our bank account…

Naturally we are in celebratory mood, it's an answer to our prayers, quite literally, and we pay off some mortgages and plan another holiday.

All this time Dad is at the forefront of our minds. And with only one treatment to go, he is suddenly feeling unwell and has been taken into hospital. Cancer of the pancreas is difficult to treat, so far Dad has reacted well to his course of chemo and we are all expecting him to be around for a few more years, but any change is a worry.

We don't know what to expect when we get to the hospital, maybe he needs to change drugs, it could be a number of things, but when I clap eyes on Dad, I'm shocked. He is lying on a bed in the centre of a small assessment ward, there are six or seven other patients, each of them pale faced through a variety of differing ailments and conditions. Opposite Dad's bed there is a mattress on the floor and an old guy sitting on it, rocking back and forth, enjoying a conversation with himself. It looks like he's wearing some sort of straight jacket.

Got to get Dad out of here, now.

As I approach him, Dad turns his head towards me. Mum, Louise, Rachael and Hugh are here, he's wearing an oxygen mask and his breathing his shallow,

"I know you like nurses Dad," I joke, "but this is a bit extreme, isn't it?"

I give him a kiss on his forehead, everyone looks stunned including me.

"We'll get you out of here straight away," I promise looking around for a nurse or doctor.

"They're all barmy in here," Dad complains struggling to catch his breath.

Taking a quick look around the ward I can see what he means, a guy in the corner is swearing and arguing with himself, another is staring vacantly into space and another wears a big smile and picks his nose.

Once a brown-skinned junior doctor has kindly promised to have Dad moved by morning we all leave to give him a rest. Mum comes out a couple of minutes later, everybody gives her a big hug, but when it's my turn I can't keep it together.

"Don't cry darling," she sobs.

Chapter 70

Early the next morning, a smiley-faced hospital receptionist confirms Dad has been moved. Great news!

But his kind-hearted specialist Atah, greets us with shocking, sobering and devastating news.

"Dad's vitals are all over the place," he tells us, "it's imperative your father gets home today," he is speaking softly and his puppy eyes give the game away, "or he may not get home at all."

I always imagined that at a time like this, you cave in, mentally and physically. Maybe it's the shock or perhaps my faith, but I remain rational and clear headed. We all know what Atah is telling us, so we do what we have to do without considering the bigger picture, simply focusing on Dad's immediate needs...

Atah is 35 or 36 years old I guess, he and Dad have forged a good friendship together, he looks upset. A fine man.

Back at my parent's home, Hugh steps up to the plate right away, presiding over seven grandchildren, selecting the downstairs room which offers the best view, organising fresh flowers and silver framed family photos to surround Dad when he's in situ. From where his bed will be, the full-length windows will give him a clear view over the kidney shaped fish pond, over the immaculate grassy lawns, and across grassy meadows that gently rise up into the far distance.

Hugh wants a comfy chaise-longue to be set beside Dad's bed so Mum can sleep next to him. By the time the ambulance arrives, everything is in place, including the oxygen cylinders and pumps.

Once Dad is installed the whole family take turns to chat with him, I can only describe the atmosphere as carnival like, the younger grandchildren swirling around the rooms downstairs, others nattering about their summer holidays, and yet there is a sombre undertone gnawing away at the edges of hope and optimism. It's hard to describe how this feels.

Danielle stays with the girls in her parent's holiday home only a mile or so away, while Hugh, Louise, Rachel and I camp down in the big room to be with Mum and Dad.

In the early evening, Hugh, with his enormous strength, carries Dad backwards and forwards to the loo. I watch him as he breaks up a sleeping tablet and pops a quarter tablet into Dad's mouth, then holds up a glass of cold water to his dry chapped lips. Louise and Rachael tuck Mum into the chaise-longue, and we all move into the kitchen to leave Mum and Dad alone. To watch them both holding hands as they drift off to sleep is gut wrenching, unbelievable and heart breaking.

It's midnight, Hugh and I take ourselves upstairs, and I lie on my bed hoping for a few hours' kip. I must have drifted off when the screams of a furious wind startle me. Windows are creaking under the great force which hurtles round and round the house. In the darkness I strain my eyes to read the blue fluorescent numerals on the alarm clock beside my bed. It's 4:04 in the morning.

The angry wind falls silent, as if trying to fool me into thinking it's disappeared or moved on. But as it strikes up again, with more force than before, it reminds me of something I read in the Bible, I think it's Luke 11 chapter 9 or Mark 21-22 or Peter 1 vs 5-8, something like that, "Your enemy the devil prowls around like a roaring lion, looking for someone to devour."

Well if he's got his eyes on Dad, he's shit outa' luck, 'cause he's on his way to heaven.

With these thoughts in mind, I tiptoe down the creaking staircase trying hard to avoid the noisiest steps.

Once downstairs, the hall lamps throw pale yellow light into the main room where Dad and Mum are hopefully sleeping. I peer through the glass doors, Louise is stretched out on a settee, and Rachael is curled up on a comfy chair. Mum still has her arm lying over Dad's chest. As I gently open the doors, nobody stirs, the humming and hissing of Dad's breathing apparatus seem to fill the whole room as I tip toe over the lush carpet to sit down next to him. I take hold of his hand.

"I love you so much Dad," I whimper. He doesn't stir, I'm shaking like a frightened puppy, muffling my voice so as not to wake anybody in the room.

For a while, maybe an hour, maybe more, I sit and watch as Dad's chest half rises and then dips in narrow unison, I can see the inside of his mask misting and then clearing as he clings on to life.

I love Dad so much, as my dad and also as my best friend, I feel sick as I listen to his lungs burbling and gurgling, I don't understand how I'm able to cope watching him die like this. I know a part of me is dying with him, a part of all of us is dying with him.

It's breakfast time when Danielle and the girls pick me up and take me back for a couple of hours. The simple pleasure of being together with them is enough to raise my spirits and boost energy levels. I am such a lucky guy.

When I get back, a nurse is giving Dad a diamorphine injection. He is restless and morale in the camp is very low.

By late afternoon, Dad is lucid but his eyes sparkle in bewilderment, I can hardly bring myself to look him in the eye without giving the game away, even now Dad senses there is some form of hope, a thread of optimism. That's who Dad is, never a quitter, the glass is always half full.

Dad's eldest grandchildren, Charlie and Sophie, turn up with a wheelchair and Hugh has the bright idea to wheel Dad into the next door room where a log fire throws shadows all the way up to the top of the vaulted ceiling.

Mum and Dad take centre stage and Hugh, Louise, Rachael and I slouch on settees and comfy chairs as we all sip champagne and talk together in mellow tones of happy memories.

When Dad begins to tire we leave him holding hands with Mum as the fire slowly reduces.

Before they married, Mum and Dad were boyfriend and girlfriend and best friends for six years. Today is their 58th wedding anniversary.

Chapter 71

Wednesday. Last night, we all sat around the kitchen table and talked candidly of our determination that Dad is not going to suffer a painful or humiliating exit. We will do whatever we have to for Dad's sake.

I pray and pray that God will take over now.

First thing this morning, Dad's wonderful palliative nurse arrives and sets him up on a new morphine dispenser. He is very weak now and asks Mum to call their local vicar, Chris, to come over for a chat.

Chris sounds delighted at the invitation, almost as if he's been waiting for the call, and wastes no time in donning a crash helmet and firing the scooter up.

Only minutes later this gargantuan man is wobbling up the gravel driveway, his scooter protesting beneath his twenty or thirty stones.

Chris is a giant of a man in every sense, he wears a distinguished grey-black beard and a short cropped, jet black hairstyle, his hand is soft to touch and he has a gentle manner about him. He stays for a couple of hours, we are all wandering from room to room in a daze, partly torn at the thought of Dad dying and partly shocked at that very prospect.

Joyce, Dad's sister, is here with us, she busies herself helping Mum and telling funny stories about Dad when he was a nipper.

"Mother used to say," she chuckles, "He was always finding something that wasn't lost," referring to the treasures he would bring back after scrambling over the rubble following bombings over London.

Joyce is several years younger than Dad, she has often been the butt of his practical jokes, he would often refer to Joyce as 'Ginger' due to her auburn hair, and one of his standard mottos was: 'never trust a ginger'. He openly admits he took a dislike to his younger sister the minute she was born, and she always howls with laughter whenever the subject comes up. Joyce seems to have a never ending collection of funny stories about her brother which are helping to drive a nail through our growing agony.

We all filter through into the room where Dad and Chris have been talking together. Before Chris leaves, he takes Dad's hand.

"Let go now, you've done everything asked of you, rest now, well done," he tells Dad before he stands up and makes his way out. I watch him disappear down the driveway wobbling on his little red scooter.

Chapter 72

Moments later, at four in the afternoon, Dad opens his eyes. They are bright aqua-marine in colour. Mum is holding his hand. Dad looks directly into her eyes for a few moments. He holds his gaze and then slowly, very slowly, gives out his final breath.

Chapter 73

10 years later…
My daily routine is one of pleasure, enjoyment and contentment. Silent prayer kick-starts the day giving thanks to Jesus for anything and everything I can think of, I take nothing for granted.

During the generous university holidays Danielle and I breakfast with Emily and Hannah around eight a.m. What a privilege and pleasure it is to share time with them.

A luxurious and healthy-style breakfast menu includes smoked salmon, avocado, toast, Manuka honey and coffee. We truly value each and every day together and max out the pleasure.

I like to clear away all business matters and administration chores swiftly. Right now I'm in a property development partnership with my brother, mother and sisters. This is no easy alliance and there's much patience involved, a lot of giving (my brother, mother and I), and a great deal of taking (my sisters...).

Now I understand, I get it, my personal knowledge of this world has come through joy, adversity, sadness and determination, in unequal measure, and without all of these experiences, the recipe of a good life would be incomplete. The dough would never rise. Much more importantly, without my faith in God and Jesus there's no kitchen, no oven, no recipe, no cake, nothing, I'm not preaching, just telling how it is for me and how it could be for you. I feel blessed.

The time is coming up to eleven a.m., by lunchtime I aim to finish this book, then to contemplate the beginning of a new book. Rowley, my trainer arrives later to help build my body in readiness for next winter's ski season in Val d'Isere where the air is clean and fresh and where we can contemplate life and appreciate how lucky we are.

My next book will be a comedy, something to put a smile on the reader's face, something to bring outrageous laughter to the daily mix of stress and pressure. And something to express my faith in God. And my love for Jesus, after all, I owe him everything.